<u>Dedication</u>

This book is dedicated to the memory of Alexander "Bou" Whyms, my best friend. From second grade until May 29, 2001, Bou was with me – through high times and hard times, fears and joys, victories and near misses, even a downright flop or two. Bou was steady, like spring rain. He was there when I was married – all three times. He helped me through my struggles as a father. He was with me when I left our native Miami for a deejay job in the cold and snow of Ohio and right there when I made my way to New York, pursuing my ill-fated splash into talk TV.

It is hard to remember life without Bou and sometimes hard to get on without that patented smile, later shining through a full white beard. He is missed, not simply because he was good. He is missed because he seemed to be permanent part of life as I knew it.

Life is different now, knowing that smile is so far away, but I thank God for preserving it in my mind's eye. I catch it from time to time, and it feels good.

Acknowledgements

This book would not have been possible without the efforts of several people whose energies and ideas I greatly appreciate. It's important to do our best and it's very important to recognize that great work happens when the whole team does its best. My thanks to the whole team.

More importantly, to my children who have been in my corner in good times and in bad. Thank you for loving me unconditionally.

Introduction

For a long time I have wanted to write a book that would serve people in the ordinary ways they live their lives. It's nice to see your book on a shelf or a coffee table, but it is even nicer to hear that people are leaving it open on the nightstand or next to the bathroom sink. It's a great compliment when someone buys your book. But when you present something of yourself to people, you hope they will actually use it, make it their own.

This book of collected thoughts has roots in various stages of my growth, both as a person and as a professional. I wanted to cover plenty of territory, so the topics are diverse. They cover a range of emotions and circumstances I have experienced either directly or through the experience of others I've known or met.

When I started getting feedback from people who had listened to my motivational CDs, I found it moving. I have heard people say that they were freed from some terrible demons with the help of one tape series or another. I learned that entertainers, parents, sales people, entrepreneurs, athletes, recovering addicts, community leaders and others had either bought my tapes themselves or had been given them by a friend. Then someone reminded me that there was a whole world of people who have not been introduced to motivational tapes, and that the written word could serve as a whole new dimension of potential impact. I like the sound of that.

If this book works as intended, you will find a thought or two that hits home for you. Maybe you will be prompted to go into action on some special project. Or maybe you'll find some relief from a burden that has been weighing you down. Perhaps some dream you have forsaken will get your attention once again. If that happens, then this effort will have been a complete success.

Since this book is dedicated to Bou, it can only meet its challenge if it is put to work. Bou worked, and his work spoke louder than his words.

Use this book, and you will help me pay tribute to a lifelong friend whose life deserves a tribute.

- LES BROWN

Contents

Why Me?

Have you ever asked yourself why some people are able to press on when trouble and difficulties in life come, while others collapse at the first sign of trouble?

I believe it has a lot to do with a person's attitude. A person with the right attitude says to himself or herself, *I may be here in this situation, but it doesn't mean I have to stay here.* When faced with a challenge, do you ask: *why me?* Or do you accept the opportunity for you to grow? Think about the last time you had to overcome a major challenge in your life and then think about the positive change that took place in you as a result of having gone through that experience.

Reflecting on my life, I can think of many situations where I could have asked this question: *Why me?* I realize then as I do now, however, that asking it would serve no real purpose to change it. By focusing my attention on the solution to the problem rather than the problem, I was able to quickly turn what seemed like a major crisis into an opportunity.

Very often when I have had people ask me this question about a challenge in their life, my response to them has been, "If not you, then who would you suggest?" Life happens to everyone, but we can be certain that IT IS GOING TO HAPPEN!

We each have the talent to take us past the circumstances and challenges life brings to propel us into our greatness. Instead of giving into the challenges and difficulties in life and asking yourself, *why me?*, embrace the enormous possibilities and proclaim, **Why not me?**

Caption: *I may be here in this situation, but it doesn't mean that I have to stay here.*

We've Got Something Special

Although not everyone realizes, each of us has something special: something unique and valuable: to contribute to society. The problem is that too often we spend so little time and effort looking at ourselves and so much time looking at other people that we never recognized just how truly special we are. When we spend our time looking at what other people do or what they have, we deprive ourselves of the opportunity to see our own value. What a trap that can be!

If I concentrate on the following some trail that is not mine, I can only come into my own by accident, thereby taking the risk of never fully realizing my potential. When I think of all of the things I dabbled in and played with, I have to be truly grateful that my love of words and my attraction to people found a natural connection.

As a radio deejay, I enjoyed entertaining people and basking in the popularity beyond what I could have wished for. But once I saw the possibilities of reaching people in more profound ways, it seemed a little silly to be simply amusing them. There were community conditions that needed to be aired, and there were people whose hopelessness I just could not ignore. I lost my job as a broadcaster, but the airways were not my only platform.

Public office became a new possibility, while serving in the Ohio House, I was invited to speak to a national organization in New Orleans. The long, loud standing ovation I received offered me a new direction. I knew right then that public speaking was the right path for me .

I have known others who found their paths earlier in life, but I did not mind that I discovered mine later. What was important was that I found it! I've known school janitors that virtually owned their buildings and mechanics who would probably pay people just for the opportunity to fix their cars because it gives them such a feeling of accomplishment. There are others like pediatric nurses who couldn't imagine not caring for babies, and grounds keepers who thrive on bringing a multi colored landscape to life. The trust is, each of these people have found their paths.

Think about what special thing you could be doing. And if you haven't already started, get to work on it. It could be something you dreamed of doing but never pursued. Figure out how you can redirect your time or energy to fulfill your special aspirations. Ask friends and family members for their input. They may see something powerful in you that you have yet to see in yourself.

Get going! We never know how much time we have left on the planet, and there are never too many people doing what you've been given to do. I promise you, you won't regret the effort, and we'll all be better for it.

The Fairness of Life in an Unfair Game

Are you the kind of person that who can handle almost anything that life throws at you? If so, then you are one of those special people who understand that it isn't about the fairness of life but rather it is about how well you can play the game.

Playing in a game when the cards seem to be stacked against you can be difficult if not impossible for some people to handle. Like most people, I can relate to feeling like this sometimes. I was dealt a serious blow a few years ago when I was diagnosed with prostate cancer.

It didn't seem fair that, after all that I managed to overcome and accomplish, this **thing** should threaten to terminate my existence. Unlike any of the previous challenges, however, this one left me speechless period. Imagine that; Les Brown, the motivator, speechless.

The question I had to ask myself was, Should I accept what appeared to be my fate, throw in my hands and die, or should I play the hand that life has dealt me, with determination and every bit of faith I could muster, and live?

I believe I am here today because I made a conscious decision to live. I have accepted that the diagnosis for the state of my health did not have to be the prognosis for my survival. I cannot predict what will happen tomorrow or the next day, but I do know that I can grasp what is before me right now. And yes, life isn't always fair, but in spite of that....TODAY I CHOSE TO LIVE!

Caption: I believe I am here today because I made a conscious decision to live.

Willing to Die For

Consider for a moment all of the important people and things in your life and ask yourself, *Of all these things, what would I be willing to sacrifice my life for?* With the exception of making the sacrifice for a child, most people would be unable to come up with a list of more than one or two.

Most people eat too much, drink too much and are stressed out too much. And if you asked them if any of these things were worth dying for their answer would be, "NO!" Yet, every day our behavior and lifestyles make a very different statement about the value we place on our lives.

I was brought face to face with this reality while coping with cancer. The radiation seed implants that I had received to treat the disease were causing major complications in my body.

In an effort to deal with some of the complications, I checked myself into a diet-based wellness center in California. This experience forced me to determine what I was willing to do in order to live. The nutrition therapy required that I give up everything that I enjoyed eating while learning a totally new approach to eating and living well. The diet at the Institute consisted of such things as wheat grass, water and vegetables. The program also required a regimen of daily exercise.

One of my favorite foods used to be fried chicken, especially wings. About three days into my treatment, I had the worst craving for just one chicken wing. I recalled that very near the facility was a fast food restaurant, and on this particular day I would have given almost anything to eat just one wing.

I had decided to sneak away when, all of a sudden, I began to think about how people like Martin Luther King, Jr. and Nelson Mandela had been willing to sacrifice their lives for what they believe in. And then I heard a voice of a minister as he made a statement about my life. He said, "Here lies Les Brown. He gave up his life for a chicken wing." The choice was mine. I could either do what I needed to in order to live, or do what I knew could take me away from here.

Think about things in your life that threaten to rob you of being able to live a healthy and purposeful life. This can be something that affects you physically, spiritually or emotionally. The question you need to ask yourself is, *what am I willing to do to have this?* If it means changing habits and lifestyles in order to change the state of your physical or emotional health, then everything you do must back up the desire to stay here.

Make an assessment of your life. Consider everything that's important to you and decide whether you could live without it. We make life and death choices every day. Some are very subtle and others more profound. The choice is simple, but to act on the right choice requires courage to change and the willingness to accept only the very best for your life.

True Measure of Success

Success isn't what you have, but who you are. And who you are can be measured in your character and in the positive impact your life has on the lives of people around you.

What guidelines are you using to measure your success? Are you influenced by what others determine to be successful or are you considering your own personal goals and achievements based on where you hope to be in life? We all experience some success each day. The fact that you got out of bed this morning and was able to put one foot in front of the other is considered a success. If you have children who love and respect you, this too can be a sign of your success.

For each goal you are able to reach, success is realized. Your success is not dependent upon whether or not it meets the standards set by someone else. Success is both very personal and relative, depending on where you would like to be in your own life.

 The realization of my own success happened when I accepted that what made me successful was far more than financial and professional achievements. So I now measure my success by the results I see in the lives of my children. The strength of our relationship is a true measure of my success as a parent. I take pride in knowing that of all the things I have accomplished, no success or honor is greater than that of being a *father*.

What guidelines will you use to measure your success? Will it be through acquiring more things, or will you strive to make a difference in the lives of people around you? Find those things that are most important to you and focus all of your attention on them. Dedicate yourself to them and the success you desire will follow each day.

Caption: If you have children who love and respect you, this too can be a sign of your success.

Getting Positive Results

To get positive results, you must cast your net in the direction of your dreams. Are you getting the kind of results you expect and want out of life? If not, then the answer might be found in how you are going after your dreams and how you spend your time and working to reach them.

In a well-known bible passage, Jesus came to the rescue of some fisherman who later became his disciples. It seems the fisherman had been fishing all day and kept pulling in an empty net. Jesus came on the scene and told them to cast their net again, but try casting on the other side. After the fisherman did as they were told, they pulled in the net to find that there were more fish than it could hold.

A true indicator of your efforts can be measured in the results of the casting you do in your life each day. For example, are you landing the big contracts? Or are you barely getting a nibble.

Suppose you are looking for a positive result for a lawn care business. You need to ask yourself, *how many lawns have I cut lately?* Are you casting your net in a neighborhood where there are lots of lawns, or are you fishing for lawn care business around the high rises of New York City?

I often speak to people who wonder why they continue to fail. In many situations, they are concentrating their efforts in the wrong places period.

Like those great fisherman of old, I must also remind myself if I want to catch fish, I must cast my net where the fish are biting. There are no short cuts or magic solutions-just a good plan, positive attitude and hard work. You can get the kind of results that you are looking for in life if you are willing to work smart to achieve them.

Caption: A true indicator of your efforts can be measured in the results of the casting you do in your life each day.

A Positive Start

Very often, the biggest hurdle in reaching a goal is getting started. And the second biggest hurdle is getting started in the right direction.

What's the first thing you think of when you wake up in the morning? Is it your problems or your goals? The funny thing about beginning your day with a problem is that it is where you will usually wind up at the end of the day.

I have learned that to get out of life what I expect, I must commit myself to beginning each day by concentrating on positive thoughts and focusing on my goals. I start each day with meditation, affirmation and prayer. I do not allow myself to be distracted by negative thoughts, negative news or negative people. This means I don't listen to the news first thing in the morning because I don't want to chance starting my day with negatives. And the same way I begin my day is how I end it. Interestingly, the two seem to work hand in hand. So, just as I begin my day with positive thoughts, I also make it a habit to end them the same way.

Whatever you think about long enough and intently enough will eventually become a reality for you. That's because your thoughts direct your actions and your actions define your life.

If you spend allot of time thinking about your problems, they'll grow bigger and stronger. Is that what you want? Of course not! Instead, focus on your goals. Start your day with them at the front of your mind, and use notes to recall them strategically throughout your day.

The good news is your thoughts are yours. They are under your control. It is up to you to use them to reach your goals and take you into your greatness.

Caption: I must commit myself to beginning each day by concentrating on positive thoughts and focusing on my goals.

Make a Plan

There is a saying that if you fail to plan, then you plan to fail. To reach your goals, you must start out with a good plan. Have you figured out how you are going to get there? To transform your goals into a reality, you must put together a road map to achieve it.

It's great to have ambitious goals. It's even greater when you can achieve them. The difference between setting a goal and achieving it is in having a good plan and working it.

How will you get from where you are right now to where you want to be? Without a solid, realistic and detailed plan, the goal is nothing more than a pipe dream. And without the commitment to follow through on that plan and put forth the necessary effort, the dream is nothing more than a good intention.

Make a commitment to begin right now to make a plan for how you intend to reach your goals. And then work your plan today, tomorrow and the next day and the day after that. Before long, the reality of your goal will become more visible and its power to pull you forward will increase. You can do it, but to make it happen, you've got to make a plan!

It's Okay to Succeed

Sometimes the greatest obstacle to success is feeling you deserve to have it. Without self-acceptance, nothing we achieve can be trusted to say with us. We see it all the time with the exploits of the rich and famous, and often we think they are different from us when they squander the fruits of their success. But are they really unlike us, or do they just have more glamour, attention and money when they go stupid?

We all go stupid from time to time, especially when we get out of synch with reality. When we get or do more than we can accept for ourselves, we all too often shoot ourselves in the foot. It's not just rock stars, actors and athletes. It happens all around us. When we produce at a higher level, we wither adjust our attitude upward or we adjust our performance downward.

I've known sales people who made breakthroughs that meant a whole new level of income. I've seen athletes run faster than they thought possible. Then they began to question themselves. What's going on here? This is too good to be true. Really! Have you ever said that? What an indictment! Too-good-to-be-true means too good for me.

As far as I am concerned, there are no overachievers. What often happens is that people achieve more than they expect, or we expect, and they don't know how to put that achievement into perspective. Here's a tip: if you made gains through your own legitimate efforts, accept them. Don't let people take you too far into the realm of applause and praise. And don't analyze success so much that you allow yourself to feel undeserving of it. It happened. Good! Be thankful! And see if you can make it happen again.

Caption: Without self-acceptance, nothing we achieve can be trusted to stay with us.

Getting It Done

There are two kinds of people in the world: those who make things happen and those who after it is done ask, "What happened?" Which one are you? Are you a spectator in your life or are you a participant?

It's easy to let things happen to you. It requires no effort, no thought, no ambition and no planning. Just sit back and wait for life to happen. The problem with accepting this approach is that life probably isn't going to be very good to you. To let things happen means to live passively, settling for whatever life decides to throw your way.

Just think about it. It's your life, although you have decided against taking an active role in living it. This doesn't seem to make much sense does it? You deserve the very best in life, which means more than just having to live with whatever comes along.

You have a choice. You can either let things happen or make things happen. Will you choose to take part in the life you're living or watch on the sidelines to see what happens?

Make a commitment today to get up, get out, get busy and get things done. You can create the life you long to have. It only requires your commitment to do it!

Getting What You Want Out of Life

How important is what you say you wan tout of life to you? And what you are willing to do or give up in order to achieve it?

This is a question that we should ask ourselves each day as we work to reach our goals. There are all kinds of goals: losing weight, getting a new car, finding a fulfilling relationship or even traveling the world. But what have you done today, yesterday or last week in order to bring your goals closer into your life?

In my travels I constantly meet people who divulge to me their goals and desires for their lives. And one of the first questions they ask me is usually, "How do I get there?" My response to them is that to get what you want out of life, you've got to be hungry for it. You must be willing to cut back or give up watching television, put in extra hours and take on the tough challenges that are bound to come as you work toward achieving your goal or dream.

Caption: ....to get what you want out of life, you've got to be hungry for it.

It is important to know what you want and be clear about it. Just as important is to ask yourself how much you want it and what are you willing to do to achieve it.

Wanting something is one thing, working to get it is quite another. You have what you need to get what you want out of life. The thing you must do is make the commitment to do whatever is necessary to get it.

Finding The Silver Lining

Life runs in cycles of good times and bad, and the only thing predictable about these cycles is that they are going to happen.

I am often fascinated by the resiliency of some of the people I meet. Life keeps knocking them down, but in what seems to be outright defiance, they keep getting up, stronger and better than before.

I suspect the reason they are able to get up is that they choose to focus their attention on good in life – what many people refer to as the silver lining.

Like most people, I have had my share of personal setbacks over the years, but each challenge presents an opportunity to do, see and live life better than before. I like to look at silver linings as the bright glimmer of hope that no matter how bad things may seem, if I continue to look up, they will get brighter.

So when life knocks you down, don't just sit there. GET UP! And remember, hard times come in cycles. Like the wind, bound by the laws of nature, they change. Hang in there!

Believing It Can Make It So

When you believe something, you've got power! Have you ever wondered why some people seem to have more control over their lives than others? It's not that they never have challenges, but they somehow are able to lead victorious lives in spite of them.

Making things in your life requires a faith, or an ability to believe that is unshakable, regardless of your circumstances.

When I was told I had prostate cancer, one of my first thoughts was, *I don't accept this.* I was not in denial, but in acknowledging the diagnosis, I had to reject the prognosis. The prognosis was that my future was threatened.

The Bible tells us that faith is the substance of things hoped for and the evidence of things not seen. I believed that in spite of the diagnosis, I would become cancer free and live whole and healthy.

My belief determined my actions, and my actions helped create positive results. Everything I did each day made a statement that I was whole and healthy, cancer free and that I expected to be here.

If you are facing a challenge, it is important that you not only live what you expect, but you must also speak it. Tell your family, your friends and everyone you meet, "I expect to be here."

Say it, believe it and receive it!

Caption: Making things happen in your life requires a faith, or an ability to believe that is unshakable, regardless of your circumstances.

Powerful Thinking

Words and thoughts are powerful tools we should use to control the experiences in our lives. For instance, your emotional state is determined by the kinds of thoughts you are thinking. If you feel down and out, nearly every reaction you have to things around you will be colored by negativity. When you have been knocked down by life, you tend to see only the worst in people, in situations and in your options. You feel hopeless. And that hopelessness really takes hold if you don't check yourself. You have to monitor your emotions.

Remember that what you are feeling does not reflect your reality! We cannot always control the thoughts that come into our minds, but we can control the thoughts that we dwell on. As Shakespeare said, "There is nothing either good or bad, but thinking makes it so." Learning to recognize emotionally distorted thinking is key to controlling your state of mind. When forced with difficult situations or hard times, anchor yourself in hopefulness rather than hopelessness, being victor rather than victim.

Allow your mind to propel you past the negative situations. Think about what you need to do and then DO IT!

Remembering 9/11

By the time the second plane crashed into the World Trade Center on September 11, I was glued to the television, watching in disbelief what was happening to New York City...to America.

Like most people, I was shaken. I was in Miami, preparing a speech I was to deliver on the 13th in Detroit. In the instant the first Trade Center building fell, that speech left my head completely. I was on the phone with my kids and others who were watching what I was watching, not saying much. Words were hard to come by.

I touched base with my office a few minutes later, trying to put myself into work mode, since I still had a plane to catch and speech to give. On one hand I was thinking, *The client expects this speech and it's under contract.* On the other hand, I was finding it hard to think about business while the faces of everyone I could remember in New York passed through my mind. As the sheer magnitude of the tragedy started to take shape, it became hard not to feel some of the deep pain. I could only imagine what the loved ones and coworkers of those missing or lost were feeling, beyond the view of the cameras.

Later, after the crash into the Pentagon and the news that a fourth plane had gone down in Pennsylvania, I began to feel uncomfortable about flying. That problem was solved for me, however, when an announcement can that all U.S. flights were cancelled for the foreseeable future. I was both relieved and stunned. I couldn't believe what I was hearing – all U.S. flights cancelled! Was this tragedy going to create such fear that the American way itself would be threatened? I guess that was the point of the attacks.

I began looking for alternate ways of getting to Detroit, including limousine services, car rentals and other means of ground transportation. As it turned out, my options had run out, but my head wasn't into business anyway. I knew that at some point I would need to find the words to help people put the events into perspective, but I was not yet ready for that role.

I began to hear a lot of comments about courage, especially concerning those who went into harm's way to save lives. But, ultimately, I was struck by the courage of ordinary people who simply would not allow terrorism to overcome them. Their fear was not as great as their grief, and their grief was not as great as their courage. They seemed to be more resigned to honoring their loved ones than to giving in to fear. They were my inspiration.

And the next time I was on an airplane, heading hundreds of miles away to make a speech, these were the people who were with me.

Many thanks to all of them.

Laughter Is Good Medicine

Anyone who knows me knows that there is nothing I enjoy more than having a good laugh. I make it my business to find situations that will make me laugh. And when there isn't anything around to make me laugh, I make something up.

Laughter to me is not a polite chuckle, but rather the kind of expression that comes up from the pit of your stomach. This kind of laughter is not only healing, but, it is one of the best ways I know to spread something good. Have you ever entered a room where everyone was laughing and suddenly you found yourself laughing too even though you had no idea what they were laughing about? What you experienced was the positive power of laughter.

There is a passage in the Bible that says a merry heart is like good medicine. In other words, it does a person good to laugh.

The next time life gets you down, remember, you have a choice. You can either stay down in the doldrums where there is nothing but more negative feelings, or you can make up your mind to laugh until the doldrums disappear. The choice is up to you. Find a reason to laugh!

Enjoying What You Do

Are you having fun yet?

I believe the saying that if you do what you enjoy, the money will follow. When I think about how much I enjoy speaking and connecting with people, it remains amazing to me that I am getting paid for having so much fun.

There is a word for working in a job day after day and hating every minute of it – insanity. When you dislike what you're doing, the tendency is to not do it very well. And doing a poor job can make you resent it even more and you send your resentment to others. The key is to guard against getting caught in that downward spiral.

Consider how much more effective you can be when you're enjoying yourself. The fact is, anything you must do can be as enjoyable as you choose to make it. And the more you enjoy it, the more effective you'll be. The most successful people in life get that way by putting passion and commitment into their work. They have learned to enjoy what they're doing, and it shows in the level of success they are able to achieve.

If you don't yet have the good fortune of being able to do what you like, then find a way to like what you do. The point is to enjoy yourself. Learn to enjoy whatever you're doing and you'll be much better at it.

You've got a job to do. Find the path to enjoyment of whatever job you have to do, and look for the opportunity to do more of the things that bring you great enjoyment – and, consequently, the success you desire in life.

Caption: There is a word for working in a job day after day and hating every minute of it – insanity.

Learning from Mistakes

I make it a habit to read two to three books a month. Reading about the lives of other achievers and their impact on our world inspires me to continue to help others realize their greatness. Interestingly, the people I read about all found their path to success as a result of making and learning from their mistakes.

When you make a mistake, you are presented with an opportunity to gain wisdom. And the only way to experience true wisdom is through your mistakes. To reach this level of appreciation, however, you must have an attitude that when you make a mistake, you will learn the lesson and move on.

If you think negatively about your mistakes, you send out a message to the universe that is filled with negativity. It accentuates the negative. "I missed one question on the exam and it ruined my day." This pessimistic approach caused you to dwell on the least positive aspects of the situation. It does not make you much fun to be around, and it adds a multitude of unnecessary problems to your life and to the lives of those who care about you. By focusing on the negative, you become a negative person. And negative people manifest negative things.

Remember that you're human, and just as you have made mistakes in the past, you will continue to make them in the future. When you make mistakes, learn to have compassion for yourself. Think of your past mistakes. You somehow managed to survive them, you learned from them and in many ways are where you are right now because of them.

Of course, you don't want to live your life purposely making mistakes. The idea is when you do make them to get the most of them. When you make a mistake don't get down on yourself. Instead, recognize it for what it is, don't hide from it or try to cover it up. Clean up the damage and try to assess what went wrong. And then transform your mistake from a negative mishap into a positive experience.

When you make a mistake, acknowledge it and then ask yourself, *what am I supposed to learn from this?* Once you have learned the lesson, grant yourself permission to move on!

Caption: ...you must have an attitude that when you make a mistake, you will learn the lesson and move on.

No Complaints

Can you imagine going through a whole day without complaining about anything? When do you think about it, there is perhaps no one who can easily meet this challenge. The reason: we are conditioned at a very young age to express when we don't like something, either through our actions or our words.

Let's examine this. Somehow does something to you that you don't like. So what do you do? Do you focus on what you don't like? Or do you turn your attention to what you don't like? Most people will automatically focus on what they don't like, even if what they don't like is just a very small part of the overall picture.

In my speaker's training and coaching seminars, I find that one of the most difficult things to help a person over come is the tendency to complain about what is wrong rather than focus on what is right. The next time you find yourself ready to complain about something, stop for a moment and think of a way replace that negative complaint with a positive suggestion.

Just imagine how powerful and positive that simple step can be in influencing your work and your relationships with other people. And think about how much it can reduce your stress.

And what about all the silent complaints you utter to yourself? Instead of letting them steal your precious time, resolve to do something about them.

When you feel a complaint coming on, step forward to take positive, productive actions instead. Use your time and energy to accomplish great things instead of worrying, placing blame or spreading criticism.

Whenever you have the urge to complain, stop right where you are. Challenge yourself to come up with a positive alternative instead. See it for the opportunity it is. This could be the chance to turn what could have been a negative outcome into a great accomplishment. Rather than looking at what you can't do, think about what you can do. Achieve something good that wouldn't have gotten done through complaining.

Tell the Truth

The truth is powerful and it pays to align yourself with it! Think about how many times you've forsaken the truth just to get yourself out of a jam. And if you admit it, you probably realize that there was always another option. Or think about the number of times you've been called on for advice or your opinion, and rather than tell people the truth, you told them what you thought they wanted to hear.

It's easy to tell people what they want to hear. It's easy to make up excuses or say something that's untrue just to get yourself out of a jam. The problem with doing this is after a while no will believe you. And once you've lost your credibility, nothing you say will matter very much at all. Do not allow yourself to get caught in that trap.

Although the truth can hurt, it's well worth the pain. When you're strong enough and confident enough to speak the truth, you gain respect and influence. Being honest and straightforward will also open doors for you. You will become known as someone who tells the truth. Think about when a statement this will make about you and your life.

Instead of covering up your weaknesses with lies, show your strength with truth. Instead of being arrogant enough to think you can get away with a lie, be confident enough to know that you CAN tell the truth.

It's important to say what you mean, and do what you say. Be honest with yourself and with others. Let your words and actions speak to the genuine and valuable person that is YOU. And then let the power of the truth set you free.

Caption: Although the truth can hurt, it's well worth the pain.

Brave Questions, Brave Answers

I believe that when most of us are asked a tough question, we are as honest as we feel we can afford to be and as dishonest as we think we have to be.

The toughest questions are not necessarily those questions put to us by other people, but rather the questions we put to ourselves. These are questions such as: *What do I really want out of life?* Or *Do I think I have what it takes in order to get it?* Or maybe you are in a relationship you might not want to be in, but you avoid asking the brave question because the answer might be too hard for you to handle. That's when you realize that partial answers and half-truths just won't do.

It takes a courageous person to be truthful during those defining moments. It requires an attitude that is fearless and willing to handle the answer given, regardless of what it might be. To live life to the fullest, you must be able to ask and answer the tough question – not only to yourself, but also to others.

Life is about being able to ask the tough questions and give the right answers. When was the last time you asked yourself a brave question? More importantly, when was the last time you responded with a brave answer? Think about it!

Act Like You Mean It

Are your actions consistent with the person you say you would like to become? If you say you want your aspirations and dreams to come true, then act like you mean it. If you talk the talk, then you need to walk the walk in order to bring your dreams to life.

The things you do will create the reality for your life. It's impossible to realize your dreams if you are doing everything to work against them. People who have achieved financial independence have been able to do so by acting like they meant to have it. Wishing will not make it so. Neither will complaining about how difficult it is. The only way to make it happen is through your positive actions; only this will make it so.

Every day of your life, you have the opportunity to mold your destiny by virtue of the actions you choose to take. The moment you start to think and act like a winner is the moment you will become a winner.

Think of what you dream about becoming each day. Have you thought about what you need to do in order to achieve it? There are no shortcuts or magic solutions – just saying and doing, saying and doing.

Your actions are the powerful tools you need to create what you say you want in life. Remind yourself each day of what you say you would like to become and then act like you mean it. And if it's yours, you deserve it.

Caption: The moment you start to think and act like a winner is the moment you will become a winner.

Priorities

You reveal your true priorities by what you do with your time and the amount of time you spend thinking about them.

What's important in your life? Is it your family, your career or a special hobby? Whether you consciously think about it or not, you have priorities. If you spend your time in front of the television every night for several hours, then watching television is a priority for you. If, on the other hand, you spend that time studying to advance your career, then your career is a top priority for you.

How you spend your time will determine where the rewards will come in your life. The things you spend time nurturing and developing are those things that will bring about the changes that you seek in your life. Priorities are the actions you take each day to make things happen.

Caption: The things you spend time nurturing and developing are those things that will bring about the changes that you seek in life.

It's easy to see what your true priorities are. Just look around you. Everything you do each day is either consciously to you. The life you live right now is the result of the priorities you set earlier in your life to bring you to this point.

If you find yourself wondering why you haven't been able to get out of life what you desire, check your priorities. Reorganize your life to spend time where it will benefit you the most.

Change your priorities and you change your life!

It's Within Your Reach

Are there things you would like to do with your life that seem virtually impossible or beyond your reach because of circumstances or obstacles?

When I look back over my life, there always seemed to be an impossible circumstance or insurmountable obstacle to keep me from realizing my dreams. But a positive attitude and a belief in myself helped me realize that virtually everything was within my reach.

It was once considered impossible for a person to run a mile in less than four minutes. But then, along came Roger Bannister in 1954, breaking the four-minute barrier and placing what seemed to be an impossible task within his reach.

It was once considered impossible for people to fly through the air or to travel into outer space. And once again, the impossible happened when in 1969 Neil Armstrong stepped onto the surface of the moon after completing the journey of a quarter-million miles through outer space. His dream of walking on the moon was placed within his reach because he and others stayed committed to making it happen.

Your impossible reaches can become your possible reaches if you commit yourself to making it happen. You can find that way through effort, persistence and an unwillingness to give up until you reach your goal

Ask yourself whether the things you think seem impossible are really impossible. Or have you made them seem impossible by not committing the hard work necessary to make them happen?

As long as you consider something impossible, it will be impossible. The only way to change it is to see the possibility in your mind, by making a decision to commit to the necessary work to place it within your reach. Your persistence and belief that it can happen will allow you to knock down the walls and remove the obstacles. And before you know it, what you once thought was out of your reach will become one of your greatest achievements.

Stretch yourself and you can reach it!

Confidence – A Positive State of Mind

Have you ever noticed athletes right before they compete? There is a state of mind that becomes visible – getting pumped – just as they are about to go head to head with their opponent. At that critical moment, all of their training and dedication to becoming an athlete will be realized if, and only if, they have the confidence that what they have been trained to do can in face be accomplished. If they lose their confidence, everything they have worked for will be lost.

It's a common problem. Most people are able to devote the time and effort required to learn or master a skill, but far too many fail to maximize their potential because they allow themselves to *choke* a critical moment. Very often, *choking* happens as a result of developing what I call "emotional reasoning." This comes in the form of excuses as to why they can't complete what they started out to do. This is usually brought on when people let their moods define what is real. They associate feeling overwhelmed with their *imagined* inability to perform. This is a very self-defeating way to think because often, if we give ourselves time to overcome our initial fears, we will discover that it isn't anything like we imagined.

To deal with this issue personally, I focus on what I am doing and the power I have within to do it. When you find yourself losing confidence, remember you have prepared for this moment and everything is working in you to help you reach your goal. Don't allow yourself to be distracted by negative thoughts that will cause you to fail.

The next time you find yourself *choking* at a critical moment, remember that you can reach your goals. Let the reasons you can win drown out any doubts. Claim the victory and make it happen.

Confidence is just a positive state of mind.

Caption: When you find yourself losing confidence, remember you have prepared for this moment and everything is working in you to reach your goal.

Thriving in Good Company

The good thing about good company is that whatever good is going n in their lives, some of it is bound to rub off on you. Hang around with the wrong people, and you'll be tainted by what's wrong with their lives.

I often think about what an important lesson this was for me to learn while growing up in Liberty City in Miami. I believe that my life would have turned out very differently had I not heeded this warning early in life. There were many opportunities for me to become involved in drugs and other situations that could have negatively impacted my life.

Hanging in good company means you have surrounded yourself with people who believe that there is so much good they could be doing, so why waste time doing bad? Good company believes in working hard and keeping an eye toward achieving the next positive goal. They have also learned that in order to manifest good, they must surround themselves with good people.

Ask yourself if you're one of the good people who successful people want to be around. Decide to be one of them, so you can attract more of them.

Dealing with Life As We Find it

We can't write the script for our lives, but we can deal with it whenever and however we find it and make adjustments in the script. Dealing with life means taking advantage of each new challenge as an opportunity to learn and accomplish something new.

When was the last time you embraced a situation that you didn't like? Did you complain through the entire experience or did you run away from the situation altogether? If you did either, you missed a wonderful opportunity to be something that you've never been before. And who knows? It just might have been that one thing that you have been wishing for.

Recently, I was invited to speak to what I thought was a large group of men on the topic of prostate cancer awareness. When I arrived, however, I was surprised to find an almost empty room. Only three other presenters and a handful of staff were there, and there was only one guest in the audience.

I had a choice. I could either leave or speak to the one person who had taken the time to show up. I didn't necessarily like what I had found in this situation, but I decided to deal with it positively anyway.

That decision turned out to be a good one. I spoke to the one person who did show up to the event and my interaction with her following the presentation turned out to be very helpful for both of us. Not only was she an important resource to know, but the staff and other presenters liked my perspective and invited me back when they could build a larger audience.

Think about ways you can handle your next situation. After all, you never know what great opportunity might be in store for you.

Dealing with life as you find it will not only get you to first base, but it will often help you to hit a home run. Seize the moment as you work your way toward your next goal!

Caption: Dealing with life means taking advantage of each new challenge as an opportunity to learn and accomplish something new.

Accepting Responsibility

It is a well-known fact that when a fish dies, it stinks at the head first. The same can be said for the heads of what were once promising organizations. Over the years, I have seen a number of situations involving best laid plans that went wrong. There always seemed to be a fair share of finger pointing to go around – one person blaming another for what was essentially his or her responsibility.

As the head of my own company, I have found over the years that whenever there has been a failure to get something done, the only person I could hold responsible was myself. Accepting the responsibility to lead means making sure that my company does what it says it will do.

There are no shortcuts doing it right. Either you do it or you turn it over to someone who can. Far too many good causes and promising opportunities have died because someone stepped up to the plate who shouldn't have.

Look at your own responsibilities. Are you handling them to the best of your abilities? Every good cause is worth a valiant effort. You must make a commitment to do what is required of you. Accept responsibility to keep the wheels of progress moving smoothly rather than slowing them down.

Live Full, Die Empty

My best friend Bou was a great cook. Among the many wonderful dishes he made over the course of his lifetime was my favorite – sweet potato pie. Bou's sweet potato pie was so good that you couldn't eat it with your shoes on, you had to take them off so you could wiggle your toes.

After speaking to a group following Bou's death, a woman at the event came up to me and said: "Mr. Brown, I have heard you speak of your friend Bou on many occasions, and you often mentioned that one day you were going to convince him to publish a cookbook with all of his wonderful recipes. I want to know, was he ever able to publish that book?" My answer to her, regrettably, was no.

It has been said that the greatest resources in the world are not found in bank accounts or in corporate structures. Instead, they can be found buried in cemeteries.

I believe that everything given to us in life is given to us as our gift to the world. "You are here in order to enable the world to live more amply, with greater vision, with a finer spirit of hope and achievement," said Woodrow Wilson. "You are here to enrich the world, and you impoverish yourself if you forget the errand."

My goal is to live life to the fullest, giving everything that I have to give. And one day, when I am done with this part of my journey, the world will say. "There went Les Brown, he gave all of himself. He lived full and died empty!"

Caption: My goal is to live life to the fullest, giving everything that I have to give.

Her Singing Is a Prayer

In the early '90's, when I was beginning to spend more time in New York, I had the pleasure of hearing a voice performance by Rachelle Farrell, an experience I'm sure I will never forget. I had thoroughly enjoyed dinner at B. Smith's Restaurant, which made me feel very much at home in ultra cool New York. After dinner with a talk show executive, we went upstairs to check out the entertainment, and we were completely blown away.

I had never heard of this young lady, but when her range started to cover the baritone and jumped to high soprano, I almost fell off my seat. What – no, who – was this? It was like no singing I had ever experienced. It was a though her singing were a prayer, regardless of the lyrics. But she didn't sing, looking pretty. She twisted her mouth this way and that, going from a deep yodel to a steady, ultrahigh note that lasted so long I had trouble getting my breath. We all – the entire room – erupted in applause after watching and listening to the vocal adventure.

The set ended with a long standing ovation. I was practically in tears. Maybe I was actually in tears. I knew I had to meet this young lady, just to tell her I thought she was absolutely amazing. She humbly accepted my praise, and told me she was a fan of mine after reading my book, *Live Your Dreams.* I was as happy as a hog in slop to talk to her, learning that my little book had been an inspiration and had helped her deal with some things in her life. We developed a friendship right away, and we still keep in touch. I began calling everybody I knew to tell them about her, harassing or begging them to go see her. In the weeks that followed, *USA Today* did a feature article on her, and a copy of the article went out from my fax machine to music lovers everywhere. What a talent!

Hearing Rachelle sent me back to the drawing board as a speaker. I knew there was more I could do with my craft, and I felt compelled to do it. I wanted my speaking to be a prayer, to honor God for allowing me the gift of connecting with people. Rachelle humbled me, even in flattering me.

And so I ask, is your work a prayer? It should be. Honor your talents, ideas and experiences by the quality of what you do.

Let your work be a prayer!

Permission to Grieve

My mother's death was as powerful to me, I am sure, as the death of anyone else's mother was to them. But, in the aftermath of saying the parting words and getting back to normal, I expected it to be very different for me. After all, I am "The Motivator."

As many people as I have coached in getting through their mother's death, I somehow felt I would be granted some immunity to the ongoing pain that comes with such a loss. Hey, I'm supposed to know this stuff! I know the stages and the process all too well from the past hours on the phone, the tears, the anger and all the rest. And yet, it wasn't coming together the way I had expected.

Somewhere around nine months or so after Mama dies, I found myself crying for no reason, feeling an intense sadness that I was sure I was through with. Hey! I've done this! I've already cried and been angry she wasn't with us any longer. I had my bouts of denial, expecting her to wake up one morning and see that it was just a bad dream. I did that already. What's wrong here?

Things were not proceeding according to schedule, at least not my schedule. I thought I was ready to move on, but I was not really ready in the deeper part of me. There was more sadness to handle, I guess. Conversations with friends in the months that followed let me know that I had my own kind of denial to deal with – that my grief was not going to complete itself on my time, but on it's own time. People I had helped began helping me, and I was grateful. I was also a bit embarrassed.

As time went by, I found myself taking time to call my brothers and sisters, and I made the trip back to Miami. It was hard to do, but I needed it. We all needed to heal. I remember going by the house in an effort to reconnect with her spiritually. Now, when I talk to people about death and dying, and about grief, it comes from a deeper understanding. I hope it helps them handle the grief. It will not allow them to skip past it.

Caption: Now, when I talk to people about death and dying, and about grief, it comes from a deeper understanding. I hope it helps them handle the grief.

Take Care of Yourself

When was the last time you did something good for yourself? I'm not referring to something major, but rather to a little thing like taking some time to meditate or walk in the park. Do you think that doing something that will bring you joy or make you feel better about yourself is being selfish?

To take care of the people around you, you must first take the very best possible care of yourself. You cannot give your best to someone else if you have nothing to give. And in order to have something to give, there must be something to draw from.

The more you take care of your own needs, the more you will have to contribute to life and to others. Taking care of your own needs does not mean having to turn your back on others. In fact, when you take the time to lift up yourself, the result will be a more positive and willing person to lift up and care for others.

As you work to better yourself through learning and improving your skills, you will begin to experience a different you – someone who is better able to make a positive difference in the world.

The choice is yours. So choose to be happy, prosperous and fulfilled and watch how you light up the world around you.

Take a look at your life and what you could do to be better and make yourself feel better. Don't concern yourself with what people around you will think about your new attitude because initially they might not understand. As a word of caution, don't be surprised by your own reaction. Remember, I'm talking about making a change in the way you think about and respond to your needs.

Do something small each day and, after each success, you will begin to see how you increase your value to those around you as you continue to be good to yourself.

Caption: To take care of the people around you, you must first take the very best possible care of yourself.

Getting to Know You

What would you say if someone walked up to you and asked, "Who are you?" Who would you tell them you are? To answer that question, you must first know that person who lives and breathes inside you. Do you know who that person is?

To be able to determine what you want in life, you must first know the person who wants it. When you know and understand yourself, you can begin to tap into the power of your own uniqueness. By understanding yourself, you allow yourself the freedom to no longer let life hold you back and find the positive energy to move on.

You are a unique individual. Think about it! Of all of the millions of people walking the planet, there is no one exactly like you. There are people who look like you and some may even act like you in certain ways, but when you consider the total you, there is only one.

The fact that you are unique can help you realize that there is something inside you that was given to only you to make a difference in this world. You cannot, however, know what that thing is unless you get to know yourself and understand what it is about you that makes your existence so unique and special.

Don't waste time trying to find yourself in other people. When you compare yourself to others or try to be like them, you deny yourself and the universe the opportunity to be blessed by the gifts and talents that were given only to you.

Your success and everything that you have to contribute in life will only come through your understanding of who you are and what you have to give to the universe.

You are destined to do great things in your own special way. You can get going by getting to know the most influential person in your life. Begin right now to discover your priceless treasure!

Caption: The fact that you are unique can help you realize that there is something inside you that was given to only you to make a difference in the world.

Live without Regrets

The secret to living a good life is to live each day with no regrets!

If you could relive the last thirty days, what would you do differently? Most people could come up with a long list of could've, should've and would've. The truth is, once you lived it, it's done. You cannot go back.

By looking back, you can determine what it was about your experiences that brought you joy and satisfaction and what happened to produce regrets. As a result, you can gain a better understanding of yourself.

When you understand yourself, you can begin to shape the situations and things around you. You will find that your behavior will become different because you understand what is needed in order to produce the results you desire.

I believe that people and situations respond to us based upon what we ask. If our language and behavior asks for what we need to be happy or successful, it will happen because we have opened up ourselves to receive it. There is a well-known passage in the Bible that says, "Ask and you shall receive." Another says, "You have not, because you ask not."

Only you can answer the question of what you need to make you happy. To ask, you must first understand who you are.

Although you cannot relive the past, you can learn much about yourself as a result of having lived it. It requires an honesty with yourself as well as a willingness to do what is necessary to live a better life.

Of all the things you can acquire in this life, the most valuable is an understanding of who you are and what role you are to play on this planet.

Caption: When you understand yourself, you can begin to shape the situations and things around you.

Strength in Weakness

People are at their strongest when they are able to identify their weaknesses! This seems almost contradictory, doesn't it? The truth is, it isn't. When you identify a weakness in your life, you've uncovered a powerful path for self-improvement.

If you work on the things at which you're already skilled, you can only make marginal improvements in your performance. Yet when you put your efforts into overcoming a particular weakness, the results can be dramatic.

Our weakest areas are usually the ones causing the greatest strain on our mental energy and ability to perform. Consider a salesperson who is knowledgeable about his or her products or services, is very good with people, is a great listener and negotiator and is skilled at closing the sale. If this same person has trouble managing the time and is always late for appointments, what impact do you think this will have on his or her performance? Chances are, that one weakness will severely restrict the effectiveness of this salesperson's overall strengths.

If we make an effort to overcome that weakness, the performance overall will increase to new levels.

What's your weakness? There is a wealth of positive results just waiting to happen; you only need to tap into it. Begin now to turn that weakness into your greatest strength and wait for the positive payoff.

Caption: People are at their strongest when they are able to identify their weakness!

Your Response

What you allow is what you get.

People will do to you what you allow them to. You may not realize it, but people could be controlling you. If your mood or response to a situation changes based upon someone's behavior toward you, then they are, in fact, controlling you.

Think about the last time someone was rude to you. What was your reaction? Did you become upset o were your feelings hurt?

The behavior of others is unpredictable. If you let another person's behavior take control of your attitude, you will begin to experience a shift not only in your behavior but also in the outcome of the important things in your life. The fact that some people will say things that you disagree with does not require you to waste your time and energy with negative behavior.

How can you stay in control of your behavior? By deciding when, if and how you will respond, based on what you want or need out of each situation. You have control over yourself, and the only way you lose that control is by freely handing it over to someone else. No one can continually insult you or hurt your feelings without your permission.

Don't allow yourself to be sucked into another person's negativity. Instead, keep in mind that the behavior of that person is their problem, not yours. Live your own life. Maintain your own sense of self and reap the rewards of living that are under your control.

Caption: If you let another person's behavior take control of your attitude, you will begin to experience a shift not only in your behavior but also in the outcome of the important things in your life.

The People Around You

If you want to move ahead in life, surround yourself with people who are headed in that direction.

Are the people around you holding you back or empowering you to move forward? If you life is going nowhere, take a look at the group of people you hang around with. You might be surprised to learn that your relationships are probably the hindrances to the goals you are trying to reach in life.

Your relationships with others can either tear you down or life you up; it depends on who they are and where they are headed in their lives. It is natural to be influenced by those people with whom you spend most of your time. So it makes good sense to determine whether these people can help to move your life in a positive direction.

Caption: Your relationships with others can either tear you down or lift you up; it depends on who they are and where they are headed in their lives.

When you spend time with people who are disciplined, ambitious, positive and effective, these qualities are likely to rub off on you. You cannot help but become more positively focused as a result.

It is important to surround yourself with people who life you up, encourage you, share your vision and inspire you. They should also care enough about you to tell you not what you want to hear, but what you need to hear.

Too get the most out of your time and your relationships, head in a positive direction!

Pushing Yourself Forward

To get what you want out of life, you must be willing and able to push yourself, even if you don't feel like it.

Expecting the best out of yourself will help you to get up early in the morning when everyone else is sleeping late. Expecting the best of yourself will keep you going even when difficult challenges try to block your way.

There are times when we want a push from someone, times when it seems tough to push ourselves. That's okay once in a while, but it's important to remember that a push from someone else is usually a push in someone else's direction. The best way to keep moving on your own path is by doing your own pushing. Others can help, but make sure they're helping to push you where you want to go, if you want to be successful.

People who are successful in life are always those who are able to push themselves. They know where they want to go and how to use what they have learned to get there.

Knowing when something is possible for you , when you expect to achieve it and when want it bad enough will give you the powerful push you need to attain your goal.

So the next time you feel you're in a "stuck" position, get up, take action and push yourself toward the things you wish to achieve in your life.

Only YOU can make it happen!

Caption: Expecting the best of yourself will keep you going even when difficult challenges try to block your way.

Reach Higher

Reach high and you will grab hold of more than you expected.

When you dare to dream big, you get big results. When you choose a big goal, you set your mind, body, spirit and resources in a positive motion to reach that goal. When you have a clear and specific goal, your efforts become focused on getting there by using every resource at your disposal.

If something appears to be out of reach, it's probably because you have not seriously put your efforts behind achieving it. Once you focus your mind on reaching a goal, you will find yourself becoming the person you need to be in order to achieve it.

When you limit yourself, you limit the possibilities in your life. By reaching beyond the obvious or easiest goals to attain, you will allow yourself to stretch to greater and greater heights with each new accomplishment.

When you convince yourself that you are only capable of doing what you have already done, you set up a pattern of mediocre accomplishments, never realizing your full potential.

If you find yourself going after things that are easy, find ways to reach beyond those invisible boundaries that you have set up in your life. Set a goal that's meaningful and compelling enough, and your skills, your knowledge and your effectiveness will expand in order to reach that goal. Reach beyond yourself and you'll find yourself growing in order to get there.

A good way to know if you are not reaching is to check your comfort level. If you are too comfortable, then you are probably not reaching.

You are greater than what you did yesterday. You can achieve more than you will accomplish today. Aim high, stretch yourself and you will be surprised at just how far you can go.

Caption: When you have a clear and specific goal, your efforts become focused on getting there by using every resource at your disposal.

Live the Adventure

Life is an adventure, filled with incredible possibilities! Shop for a moment and think about what it means to be alive. You can sense, you can breathe and you can create. You can inspire, you can challenge and be challenged. You can make decisions and reason. You know joy and can be filled with laughter.

So the question is: Are you taking your life for granted? Are you allowing your days to be consumed with boredom and frustration? Time is your most precious gift, not to be dwindled away in idleness or negativity.

Take a look around you. There are countless places to be explored, people to meet, things to be learned and challenges that will enrich your life and the lives of people around you. If you could live a thousand lifetimes, you would never run out of reasons to live an exciting and productive life.

So instead of wasting your life, live it! Start each day with a fresh outlook. Make a commitment to yourself to learn something new and do something different each day. Not only will you experience a personal transformation, but the people around you will be transformed as well.

Silencing the Doubts

When was the last time you spent your doubts packing? Believe it or not, your doubts are keeping you from living the rich and fulfilling life you deserve.

Each time you listen to that little voice inside that says *I can't* or *It's not possible*, you erect roadblocks in your life. Think about it. You set ambitious goals or make great plans, and suddenly that little voice begins to whisper all the reasons why you can't do it, causing you to doubt, stopping you cold.

The key to getting rid of that little negative, nagging voice is to understand where it comes from. It is a monster that you yourself have created. You've told yourself, or have been told by others, *No, I can't* so many times that your doubt has taken on a life of its own.

You created that little voice of doubt. And because you created it, you have the power to silence it.

Caption: The key to getting rid of that little negative, nagging voice is to understand where it comes from.

Each time that little voice tells you, *No I can't*, answer with *Oh, yes I can!* And then go one step further by doing it. Tell yourself, *I am worthy, I am willing, I am prepared and yes, indeed, I can certainly do it!*

And when the voice of doubt comes from within our homes and from those around you, you have the power to silence them, too. Remember, only you can control what you believe and don't believe. You can either accept the doubt or reject it.

Silence the doubt. Live the life you deserve!

Turning In

When you really tune in to the world around you, good things happen.

Have you ever noticed that when you buy a new car, suddenly you see that same model everywhere you go? Did that model become popular simply because you bought yours? The answer of course is no. What happened was you suddenly became more aware of all of the vehicles like yours that were already out there.

The same thing happens when you commit to achieving a goal. When you make a solid commitment suddenly the opportunities and resources necessary for reaching that goal become visible to you.

Whatever you seek in life, you will find. If you are not in tune to those things that you either want or need, you will miss then every time. That is why it is important to stay focused on your goals, to be able to recognize them when they appear. Staying focused allows you to see good things when they come to you. Because you are focused, everything about you is ready to receive what the universe has prepared for you.

Committing to a goal will not only open your eyes, but you will begin to see the value in everything that happens to you – the good things and the bad. You will understand that each experience serves as a pathway to help you reach your goals.

You can find what you need to be successful. You can achieve your goals. But you must tune in. And then stand back watch as the miracles in your life unfold.

Caption:....it is important to stay focused on your goals, to be able to recognize them when they appear.

Your Good Fortune

What would you say to someone if they asked you to identify your most valuable possession? And what would you do to celebrate if you suddenly found out that because of that possession you are now rich beyond your wildest dreams?

Now consider this. You have something far more valuable than the most expensive thing you can imagine. And no matter how much money you acquire, it would be impossible to replace it.

Your good fortune is your life and you have this day in which to live it. You are special. There is no person in this entire world quite like you. And if you searched the entire world over, no one could ever replace you.

So how will you celebrate your good fortune? Will you waste this day and everything in it? You are worthy of the best life has to offer; it is yours for the asking. You live in a world filled with abundance and opportunity. Will you allow your good fortune to pass you by?

Forget about what you don't have and focus on what you do. You are a wealthy human being, filled with life, waiting to receive the good fortune that life has prepared for you.

Fortune has indeed smiled on you. And now, it's up to you to claim it!

Caption: There is no person in this entire world quite like you. And if you searched the entire world over, no one could ever replace you.

Earning the Support Of Others

When you provide something of value to others, you always get more in return.

Who stands to gain more from your achievement than you do? Did you know that one of the keys to achieving success in life has more to do with what you do for others than what you do for yourself?

It's a simple yet powerful concept. The way to have what you want is to help others get what they want. By providing service and value to others, you lay a foundation that is sure to result in your achievement and lasting success.

Think about successful businesses or individuals you know. Now ask yourself, *What key ingredient do they have in common?* Chances are they have the proven ability to consistently provide true value to other people. When you give to others, you provide them with something that is positive. And when you give something positive, positive results are what you will get in return.

Are you seeking to gain the support and cooperation of others? They think of ways in which you can provide something of value to them. When you extend a helping hand, people will line up to assist you in your efforts, thereby helping to move you forward toward reaching your goals. You become a magnet for good things.

You can begin your path to success right now. Make a list of successful people who can help you get where you are trying to go. And then go one step further by listing ways in which you can be of assistance or value to them.

You are now well on your way to achieving the success you have been seeking.

Caption: Did you know that one of the keys to achieving success in life has more to do with what you do for others than what you do for yourself?

Taking the Next Step

How often do you have a moment of inspiration to do something and then have that idea stall or never happen because you fail to follow through? Millions of good ideas and dreams go unfulfilled because people are not willing to take the next step.

Once you set a goal, it is absolutely vital that you immediately begin taking the necessary action to reach it. To sit on an idea or fail to act on a goal is not really goal-setting, but wishful thinking. The best idea in the world is worthless unless you do what is necessary to see it through.

The sooner you take action, the more success you'll have in reaching that goal. By taking immediate action, you make a solid and unmistakable commitment to reaching the goal. Thinking about it won't make it happen; neither will dreaming about it. The only way to make it happen is to act upon it.

Take that next step by determining where you would like the goal to ultimately lead you. Once you see yourself having reached that goal, then work backwards. Ask yourself, *What must I do in order to get where I would like to go?* Plan your moves step by step, with a commitment to work the plan until each step has been completed.

And then do it. Take the next step then move on to the next one. The only thing holding you back is you.

Commit yourself. Get out of your own way and follow your path to success.

Caption: By taking immediate action, you make a solid and unmistakable commitment to reaching the goal.

Exercising Self-discipline

Are you a disciplined person? Can you control your action, regardless of what is going on around you? When you hear the word "discipline" do you immediately think of punishment? The fact is, discipline is only punishment when imposed on you by someone else. When you discipline yourself, it's not punishment but empowerment.

If you can control your own actions, you have what it takes to be disciplined. It's a powerful tool, available any time you decide to use it. It takes a lot of effort, but the payoff can be enormous.

Discipline is the key to accomplishing things out of the ordinary. Consider the life of an Olympic gold medalist. This athlete is able to reach such heights because of years and years of discipline. It could not happen otherwise.

Discipline is a necessary part of living. The question you must ask yourself is whether you will empower yourself or allow yourself to be punished by others.

The choice is yours. Choose to be disciplined and reap the rewards!

Something to Look Forward To

Do you wake up each day with anticipation for what's in store for you? Have you made plans for a memorable getaway as a reward for your hard work?

How would you approach this day if you knew you were leaving tomorrow for a month-long vacation to a tropical island resort? Chances are no matter what came your way, nothing would be able to get you down.

The truth is, when we have something positive to look forward to, our attitude and approach to life is very different. We tend to keep things in perspective, recognizing that in most instances the problems in our lives are only minor inconveniences rather than major catastrophes. When you know there is a rewarding experience in store for you, you can endure just about anything.

Caption: When you know there is a rewarding experience in store for you, you can endure just about anything.

If there's nothing in your life to look forward to, even the most pleasurable task can seem like a major chore.

Life is about looking forward to the rewards in life. Hard work and minor setbacks are just a way of getting there.

Plan a reward for yourself in the future and you'll improve your outlook on life in the present. Commit

There is a light at the end of the tunnel. Open your eyes wide enough and you will see it.

Get on the Treadmill

One of the things you come to appreciate after turning 50 is the value of exercise. You shouldn't have to live a half-century before you figure out that your muscles, joints and blood need to move to stay healthy. On the other hand, I know people who seem to think life's ultimate treat is to be able to do nothing, and they want to get in some practice.

Unfortunately, the body doesn't operate on that logic. It seems to be saying *use me now or lose me later.* It may have taken a while, but I got it...finally! One of my first gestures of getting into shape was the purchase of a treadmill – beautiful thing too. It had bright red buttons and a variety of settings, automatic or manual – take your choice. I shopped around for a good price, arranged for the delivery and waited anxiously for it to arrive. I wouldn't need to go to the gym. I was getting my own gym, or at least a great start.

I was out of town when the miracle of technology arrived, but I heard all about it. It was being set up for me, so that I could get going as soon as I got back. Wow! My very own treadmill. I would be getting into such great shape, losing several pounds, the whole deal. I was ready.

When I got home, I couldn't wait to try it out. I would start out by walking. Then I would jog. And then I would run like the wind. I used to be pretty fast when I was younger. I would burn that treadmill up. They would have to fix the motor on that thing. Good thing I had that warranty.

I started out slowly enough, but I didn't bother to stretch. I just wanted to ru-uuunn. Unfortunately, when I got up to just about full speed, my body just wanted to sto-oop. It wasn't so painful in my legs at first. It was mostly my chest. It felt like it had heavy things stacked on it, very heavy things. Lucky for me, my breathing started returning to normal after awhile. Not so lucky on the legs, as I recall. They had apparently been truly offended. They got stiff as I moved to get up, and seemed unwilling to help me get myself into the shower. They were apparently not happy with me at all.

When I woke up the next morning, I had forgotten about my instant exercise program from the day before. My legs, on the other hand, had not forgotten a thing. My first movements of the morning were quick to remind me of the treadmill experience, and I had ugly words in response.

Later, I found myself talking with a good friend who exercises regularly, and she had a good laugh at my expense. Stretching, warming up and starting out gradually were her words of wisdom for me. I told her I was not going near that treadmill for a while, and she had herself another laugh.

As time went on, the treadmill began to take on a new role in the house. Clothes and other items could be found hanging from it or stacked on it, wasting the beast's opportunity to hurt people in the name of fitness. I finally came around though. My waistline and my stress needed what that object in the corner could provide.

I started taking my friend's advice, beginning gradually, warming up, stretching my muscles and so on. And after following a regimen for several weeks, it worked. That meant I had to find new space for the things that had found a home on the treadmill.

So Investing in that machine worked out after all. In fact, I highly recommend treadmills. One little detail to remember, though. You'll have to actually get on the thing to get results. Sorry.

Caption: You shouldn't have to live a half-century before you figure out that your muscles, joint and blood need to move to stay healthy.

Get off the Treadmill

Sure, treadmills are great for exercising, but sometimes we can end up on one of life's treadmills without even knowing it. And that can be unhealthy for both our mental and physical health.

That happens when we find ourselves running through life on an automatic, unable to enjoy the ordinary things others take for granted. If we don't watch out, we can get so caught up in making a living that we have no real to live. I can remember being so attached to the telephone, trying to make business deals happen, that I missed some great opportunities with the kids.

I wouldn't have called myself a workaholic, but I can remember thinking that the telephone was so important that I couldn't afford to miss even one call – not even with an answering machine or electronic voice mail backing me up. I found out that being that accessible and that busy is a recipe for chaos. Why have a staff if you don't trust them to keep you up to date, on schedule and properly prepared?

A wake-up call from one of my kids finally put everything into proper perspective. Big events happen, bringing us in touch with the sorrow and the joy of life. We get shaken into a new sense of priority, and the quality of our lives looks more like the sum of special moments than the sum of late-night and weekend meetings or monthly minutes on the cell phone. We need the routine of tasks, memos and meetings to make things run smoothly. What we can't do is lose sight of what the work is all about.

When we find ourselves rolling along on a treadmill of our own making, we need to stop it. If it's one of somebody's else's making, we need to find way to get off. Sometimes we need to just set our feet and jump.

Caption: We need the routine of tasks, memos and meetings to make things run smoothly. What we can't do is lose sight of what the work is all about.

Pass It On!

When I see people wandering through life aimlessly, I like to ask the question, "What are you going to do with that stuff you've got?" It matter, you know. Your genes, your experience, your ideas, your talents and passions - they combine to dorm some stuff that is uniquely yours.

No one has what you have, not exactly what you have, and that makes the question all the more important. If you are uniquely qualified to act on your special stuff, what is it we will miss, if you sit there and let it languish and fade into nothing?

If we miss your painting, your poem, your song or your leadership, perhaps we'll all suffer. If you decide that your deep passion to serve or create or develop some special thing is not that important, who knows what contribution, what gift we might all be denied? Imagine the teacher, scout leader, Olympic runner, firefighter, coach or singer who touched your life in some special way. Then imagine life without the commitment it took to produce this example of humanity that you admire and appreciate.

So what are you going to do with that stuff you've got? Do you have a plan or an idea? I have a suggestion: develop it and pass it on. Make the commitment to do what is required, whatever it might entail, and keep that commitment. No excuses accepted. Your efforts are a legacy in the making, and what you don't do is being written as well.

Seize the opportunity in front of you. Use it to develop your greatness and let the lessons you learn be part of what you pass on to theirs. So do good work, and help others do theirs when you can. The world needs your best. So do your best, and pass it on.

Caption: Make the commitment to do what is required, whatever it might entail, and keep that commitment. No excuses accepted.

Escape the Trap

Most people never escape the traps in life because they fail to recognize the exits. Do you feel like you're trapped in a situation with no way out? You may have many more options than you realize.

No matter how desperate the situation may appear, you always have choices. Too often when there's a very difficult decision to make, it's easier to pretend that the choice does not exist. If you would just take a moment to step back from the situation, you would realize that by facing it head on, you can quickly put the experience behind you.

When you fail to deal with a situation, very often the problem grows far beyond what it would have been had you dealt with it at the moment it happened.

How many times have you heard of someone declaring bankruptcy when other choices were clearly available? In most cases, the only thing standing between bankruptcy and another option was a few hundred dollars. The same can be said for crimes, which often occur because people get desperate, feeling that the only option they have is the one that finds them breaking the law. As a result of not considering other options, a temporary problem is dealt with through a permanent solution.

When you are facing a different situation, never tell yourself that you have no other choice. If you tell yourself this often enough, pretty soon you will start to believe it. This kind of thinking leads to irrational and unproductive actions, resulting in an unnecessarily stressful and difficult life.

Think about what you would tell someone else if they were in the same situation. You might be surprised at your ability to think clearly when the situation involves someone else.

You are always given choices, but it is up to you to find and take advantage of them. You don't have to trapped. Look for and find the escape.

Caption: When you fail to deal with a situation, very often the problem grows far beyond what it would have been had you dealt with it at the moment it happened.

Get Going

Sometimes life can seem overwhelming. Everywhere you turn, there's work to be done. It's usually during these times that, in spite of the long list of things to do, the biggest challenge is to simply get going.

That's when it's easy to just give up, throw in the towel, because it seems like life is too much to handle. This is the time to garner your strength and move in the direction of your goals. Allowing yourself to worry, complain or avoid the situation altogether will only make it worse.

Begin by doing what you can. No matter how small the effort, one step at a time is all I really takes to turn that overload into manageable tasks.

Focus on what you have to do and you'll forget about being overwhelmed. There will always be challenges in your life. Just remember, challenges won't hurt you unless you allow them to. Learn to see the good in life's challenges and live victoriously through them. Do what you can, when you can and however you can.

You can get going. You can master that overload. But you must get up, put one foot in front of the other and boldly tell yourself, *I am going!*

Believe in Your Own Dreams

If you have an idea to do something, don't be surprised if someone tells you it can't be done. Many plans are interrupted or derailed because people share a dream or an idea and then listen to the negative feedback of people who convince them that it cannot be accomplished.

One of the biggest mistakes you can make is to fall into the trap of needing the approval of other people. Don't try to get everyone to buy into your dreams. Instead, keep them to yourself and work on them until they come to fruition. Approve your own dreams rather than waiting for someone else to do it for you.

You have the power to be the captain of your own ship, the master of your own destiny. Whether or not you reach your goals is totally up to you and does not depend on the approval of someone else.

No one knows your dreams and aspirations like you do. Only you have the passion and drive to see your dreams come to life. Another person may be able to understand the concept but because they don't have the direct insight, they won't be able to imagine the possibilities for how far you might go.

Remember, you judge a tree by the fruit it bears, not by its name. Do it!

Unleash the power to begin right now and live your own dreams.

Caption: Whether or not you reach your goals is totally up to you and does not depend on the approval of someone else.

Travel In Good Company

Misery loves company and so does success. Be aware of the company you keep. There is an old saying that even if you have an ocean of pure milk, it can be turned into poison with just a few grams of sour curds.

The thoughts, words and actions of others can influence us for better or worse. The company of those with limited vision of themselves will poison your sweetest dreams. The company of those with expanded vision will inspire you, uplift you and keep a light on your path.

Vices are contagious but so are virtues. In the company of thieves, our thoughts turn to theft, but in the company of saints, we become more saintly.

Seek out those whose qualities you admire and their qualities will become your own. Read great success stories and biographies and be inspired to begin to live a great story of your own.

We become what we behold, for what we behold becomes the very vision of ourselves. The company you keep can help you live your vision.

Maintaining Peace of Mind

Did you know that you mind can either be your worst enemy or your greatest friend? Your mind is a powerful tool for interaction. It has the power to build or to destroy. Your mind can be used to create and turn thoughts and ideas into reality. Make it strong by focusing that power. Keep it pure by constantly turning bad thoughts to good.

So how can you harness that power to give you the life you desire? Here are three important methods for maintaining peace of mind:

First, become the conscious observer of your thoughts. When your mind becomes agitated, reflect on the source of that agitation and then eliminate it. Anything that is a constant source of stress and irritation in your life isn't worth having.

Second, break the habit of negative thinking. Rather than seeing yourself as weak and limited, open up the tremendous reservoir of power and potential that comes from a disciplined and positive mind. Positive thoughts will give way to tremendous breakthroughs in your life when pushed in the right direction.

Third, treat your mind like a good friend. Schedule periods of rest and quiet introspection during which you allow yourself to perceive your thoughts as pure energy.

Above all, become a student of the sky, a giant oak, or the tiniest seed.

And remember, the peace of the universe is at your command.

Caption: Your mind can be used to create and to turn thoughts and ideas into reality. Make it strong by focusing that power.

My Own Health Bulletin

For quite some time, I have been conscious of my health, partly because of pure vanity and partly because I'm not ready to leave this life. I have been taking medication for high blood pressure for a number of years, and I've had physical blood pressure for a number of years, and I've had physical exams of one kind of another on a fairly regular basis. I've always been told that my health was good, and as long as I kept on top of my blood pressure, watching my weight and taking medication, I was good to go.

Not only have I been conscious on my own health, I've been on the case with my friends to see that each one takes proper care of that only body they will never have. As a way of showing my support for the much-discussed prostate issue, I asked others to joining me in getting a prostate exam. I figured I would lead by example, to get other men, especially African American men, checked.

All of this was taking place as I was making a plunge back into radio, very familiar for me, and paying close attention to a troubled marriage. I was eager to walk the talk on the issue of getting people involved in their own health care. As it turned out, it wasn't just the others who needed the exam. I got the news a few days later that I had prostate cancer. I was stunned. What? Me? All I've for is a little blood pressure problem, not cancer. There must be some mistake, I thought. No mistake.

The news put me in an emotionally tight position, and the issue in the marriage would have to take a back seat to the issues in my body. I needed to focus on matters of life and death. I could handle a broken heart. A broken body was something I had to face with Mamie Brown determination. I filed for divorce. Then I called together a close circle of family and friends for guidance, prayer and whatever support they could give.

In the weeks that followed, I had radiation treatment to handle the physical aspects and then took matters to God. I believe you can trust doctors to do their best, but I wanted care that only God's hand could give. I have always been a person of faith, but just in case my stock wasn't high enough in God's eyes, I took great pains to beg like I was a stranger in church. I promised everything I could think of. I joined churches I had never heard of. I increased my contributions to the collection plate, and sang louder than anybody else, trying to cut a deal.

Finally, through humility and quiet prayer, I got some peace and settled into my faith. I renewed my commitment to my health, eating the foods that could do me the most good, getting back to exercise, and staying in close touch with people whose energy helped me feel empowered. I also recognize that I was operating on a higher spiritual plane.

I decided to renew my commitment to helping people cope with the storms of life and celebrate their own unique gifts. It was the spring of '97 when I got my bad news. My good news has been coming ever since.

It's Your Future

What does the future hold for you? Have you ever noticed how some people are content to let the future happen while others make it happen? What is the crucial difference between the two?

People who let things happen have shifting priorities and shallow commitments. Typically, these people are passive, rather than assertive. They usually react rather than act, losing sight of future goals in the flux of current events.

People who make things happen keep a pure and undiluted vision of a goal and prepare for the unfolding future with a meticulous plan put into daily practice.

Think for a moment of the future as a distant city and planning as a map. If you wanted to go to that city without a map, it could take you a very long time. It is possible that you could never reach your destination.

But if you had a map or a plan of action, you could go there easily. In the same way, if you plan for the future, you can reach your goals.

It's a matter of knowing where you want to go and having a good plan to get you there.

Embracing Change

From the Bible or Koran, we are told that from the beginning of creation, change is a fact of life. And yet most of us fear and resist change. We want to crystallize a moment, a situation, a relationship or an idea and stay tooted in that reality.

But look closer and you will see that change is the ultimate reality. Everything has its season and just as a flower goes from seed to bloom, into seed again, we will and must constantly change.

Just as a child constantly adapts, grows and creates, molding reality in varying ways, we must anticipate change in our lives, our jobs and in our relationships.

Rather than reacting negatively to change, embrace it and pursue it. We can do it if we see within ourselves reflections of everything that has been and everything that will ever be.

Embrace change and make it your own.

Looking up In Adversity

Don't let life get your down. Are you going through some major challenges in your life right now? You have comeback power in you.

In order to get there, you must do a few things however. Maintain your perspective. Be aware that whatever you are going through, however difficult it may be, it has not come to stay; it has come to pass. You are greater than any circumstance that you are now facing.

A good friend of mine thought her world was crashing down around her when the company she had dedicated herself to for nearly 30 years decided to let her go. Unfortunately, not only was she being terminated, but she was given only a few minutes to clear her desk as security watched then escorted her from the building. Her only fault was getting caught in a major downsizing. After she recovered from the initial shock, she made a conscious decision to cut her period of grieving short and make a move into a new field. With sheer determination, she made a successful move into real estate sales, turning her potential negative energy into powerful, positive results.

Keep your head clear and your heart open for guidance and support. And by all means, don't panic! Expect things to get better for you. You are not alone. You have the power to overcome anything that you are now facing. And remember to look up to find your blessing.

Caption: You have the power to overcome anything that you are now facing. And remember to look up to find your blessing.

The Key to Greatness

Pursue knowledge and greatness will pursue you. There is a direct link between what you know and the unfolding of your potential. From artists to scientists, from world leaders to leading entrepreneurs, and from great competitors to great healers, we've been inspired by geniuses of unlimited horizons. And like men and women of destiny, we too can nurture our own seeds of greatness.

Concentrate with intensity of your goal. Work to master your chosen subject. If an artist, perfect the mechanics of your art. If a scientist, thoroughly search the area of your interest. If a writer, become skilled in the use of language.

Pursue your goal of excellence passionately. Whether this process takes months or years, the knowledge will prepare you for insight, revelation and greatness. The greater your mechanical excellence and the more massive your knowledge, the greater the probability that genius will express itself through you.

Your potential will show up in the knowledge you acquire and your persistence in putting that knowledge to work for you. Put your mind and knowledge into action and watch as your future unfolds right before you.

Expand Your Life

Maybe there's more to your life than you've been living. You're more than a cultural stereotype, more than an advertising myth. Young or old, black or white, think or fat, rich or poor. You're more than a label, a handle or a statistic. You are unique! You deserve a lot more. How then do you break free and live life full-measure, rich with joy and promise?

Find your purpose in life and then live it. See the core of your being as a warm and radiant source of goodness, happiness and love. It will magnetize and you and attract people, resources and events that will enrich and expand you.

Have faith in your own divinity. You are smaller than the smallest and greater than the greatest. You, in and of yourself, are a multitude!

Caption: See the core of your being as a warm and radiant source of goodness, happiness and love.

Don't Fear

You can overcome fear.

Like a mirror that is cracked in a thousand places, fear keeps us from seeing who we really are. We feel cut off, isolated, contracted and small, diminished in power and self esteem. But there are ways to conquer fear and to act from a position of wholeness and strength.

Know that you are the successful, beautiful and courageous manifestation of creation billions of years in the making. See yourself as a part of a grand and purposeful design.

Identify the sources of fear in your life. Visualize a higher you, handling those fears in a healthy and productive way.

Make a conscious effort to let go of fear and act from a sense of consciousness that will empower and protect you.

You are strong. You are greater than the fear!

You Are Worthy

You deserve more. Every day we live our beliefs. If we see ourselves as unworthy, our lives will be filled with pain. If we believe that we are inferior, we will live as slaves.

Ultimately, if you believe that you deserve more, you have the power of transformation in your hand. Your mind is so powerful that it is the greatest predictor of reality.

Just as Rosa Parks believed that she deserved to sit at the front of the bus on that fateful day in 1955, each of us has the power to live with dignity and self-respect, based on the force of our convictions. I believed I deserved to be heard, and I began a speaking career to touch the lives of people who had given up on themselves. I wanted to be a force for positive change, and I felt I deserved it.

You deserve more – more success, more joy, more peace, more health, and more wealth than you may have ever dreamed possible. You deserve more from life.

Accept it! You are worthy.

De-Stress Your Life

You can turn stress into useful energy. A little of it is a good thing. Too much of it can kill you. It can be responsible for anything from premature hair loss to heart attacks. But there are ways to convert your stress into a powerhouse of self-directed energy.

Here's how. Discipline your thoughts. Develop the mind's muscle by focusing on higher ground.

Master the art of breathing. Sometimes we become so agitated by a constant barrage of undirected thoughts that our very breath and heartbeat become irregular and stressed.

In these times, become very still. Empty your mind. Simply listen to the sound of your breathing and become focused in that healing stillness.

Balance your life with adequate relaxation and exercise. A strong and healthy body and relaxed mind can redirect stress into useful action.

And don't forget to breathe!

Caption: A strong and healthy body and relaxed mind can redirect stress into useful action.

Setting a New Standard

Years ago, while home visiting my mother, I stopped off to get a barbecue sandwich on the corner. The vendor turned around, picked up a detergent bottle with the label still on it and proceeded to pour the barbecue sauce all over the sandwich I had just ordered.

I took the sandwich and paid him for his trouble, but I couldn't help but think about where his head must have been – the standards that he has set to achieve the things that he wanted for his life.

I realize today, that in order to make it you've for to have certain standards that you should adhere to. I also realize that it doesn't take an Einstein to move from where you are to where you want to go. But many of us are so locked into being mediocre that we miss the best that life has to offer us, like an endless line of customers, waiting for our barbecue.

John H. Johnson, founding publisher of *Ebony* magazine, said something that's very important if you want to make it today: "There is no defense against an excellence that meets a pressing public need." Find a need and fill it by providing high-quality service, and I guarantee you'll become successful and set the new standard.

Are you setting a high standard for your life? If not, make the commitment necessary. Don't just dabble.

Do what you do to the highest level possible. Set a standard we'll all want to talk about.

Caption: ....many of us are so locked into being mediocre that we miss the best that life has to offer us.

You Deserve It

I want to give you three basic steps to a better life. Here's how you can turn your life around.

First, think about something that you want to do and believe within yourself that you can do it. See, you never get a strong idea without the corresponding talent or ability to make that idea or dream become a reality.

Second, believe that you deserve your dreams. People don't do any more than you're doing in life because in their subconscious they don't believe they deserve any better. You've got to say to yourself every day, *I deserve my dream.*

You've got to go into action. If you just dream about it and think about it and feel that you deserve it but remain unwilling to invest your time, energy and resources to make it happen, nothing is going to come forth for you.

Having your dream is about conceiving it. Living your dream is about doing it. You have the power within you. Live your dream!

If you want to make things happen in your life, if you want to do something exceptional or different, you've got to learn to live with criticism. In fact, if you want something really big to happen, you need to learn to embrace the kind of criticism that can help you go from where you are to where you want to be.

Lots of people give up on their dreams or never make a serious attempt, because they are afraid of criticism. They identify with the feedback they get, rather than identifying with the possibilities if they effectively utilize the criticism to make things better. We all know people who seem to take special delight in walking on others' dreams. People who don't have big plans for their own lives often try to prevent others from leaving them behind.

People who succeed are those who keep caring critics close at hand, and dismiss the dream busters from their inner circle. If you do a good job of listening, you can make strategic corrections that you might now know about, except for good criticism. On the other hand, when you limit the exposure to negative voices, you empower yourself to take on the real challenges – those that come from the work itself.

You have things to do with your life, and your most important critic should be you. Only you can determine where your life should be going. Let others help you figure out how to get there. But it's your idea, your dream, and it's up to you to live it.

Caption: People who succeed are those who keep caring critics close at hand, and dismiss the dream busters from their inner circle.

Giving It All You've Got

You can't hold anything back if you want to live your dreams.

Many of us never reach our goals in life because we go after them halfheartedly. It's tough to climb the ladder of success, especially if you're trying to keep your nose to the grindstone and your shoulder to the wheel, your eye on the ball and your ear to the ground. You've got to put everything you've got into it.

Someone once said that all you can do is all you can do and all you can do is enough. But make sure you do all you can do.

Most of us never realize our true greatness in life because we don't do all that we can do. If you decide to make your dream a reality, just remember you've got to give it all you've got. And all you've got it enough!

Capture: It's tough to climb the ladder of success, especially if you're trying to keep your nose to the grindstone and your shoulder to the wheel, your eye on the ball and your ear on the ground.

Staying Ahead Of the Game

If you don't keep doing it better, your competition will. You know things are changing so fast that, to make it today, you've got to work constantly to develop yourself and find ways to do what you're doing even better. If you don't, somebody is going to overtake you.

That's how I found my niche in motivational speaking. I looked around at various speakers, and they were giving memorized, canned speeches. I decided to become well-read and to research all the subjects I would speak on so I could speak with authority. And as I began to pursue that, I realized my only competition was me.

Most other speakers wouldn't invest the time and energy to get better. That gave me another advantage, because I've never been satisfied with myself as a speaker. I keep working to get better and better. Make that your edge; whatever you're doing, never become satisfied with yourself. Always realize that you can get better. Your best work has not been done yet. Practice! Practice! Practice!

The Power Of Working Together

A key element you need in your life if you want to make your dream come true is someone who shares your vision, someone who had bought into your dream.

It has often been said that two people who are united in life, working toward the same goals and dreams, can achieve more than one person. I know that from my own life, overcoming financial hurdles, low expectations other s had of me , and the challenges all newcomers face when they have no previous experience. There is no way I would have been able to become a successful deejay and broadcast manager, win three terms in the Ohio legislature, win the highest award offered by the National Speakers Association, be presented on public television, become the author of successful self-help and support of people who believed in me.

If you don't have the support right now, don't stop until you find it. It will give you that extra impetus you need to achieve your goals. You can go far with your own determination. You will go furthest with support.

Remember, behind every great person is someone or some team who shared and believed in their goals.

Living Fully

Thomas Carlyle once described people who would never consider committing suicide yet thought nothing of dribbling their lives away in useless minutes and hours every day.

He was talking about the living dead. It's worse than suicide. These people have no drive, no ambition, nothing they're working toward. They are cynical, negative and highly critical.

A friend of mine is a very talented singer, a crooner who I've seen have his way with audiences on more than one occasion. He looks the part, and he can sing a ballad in a way that only a gifted singer can. I can't mention his name, but even if I did you wouldn't know who he is. He has led such a self-destructive life that efforts to promote his career have not gotten very far. He has so much potential that I keep trying to bring his stuff to life. Unfortunately, it's really up to him.

If you're among the living dead, decide today that life is God's gift to you, and how you live your life is your gift to God.

Give a good gift!

Facing Change

"Not everyone that is faced can be changed, but nothing can be changed until it is faced."   -JAMES BALDWIN

Many of us are in relationships or circumstances in our lives that make us unhappy, even miserable, but we haven't developed the courage to face the truth and to take action to change it.

Life is too short to go through it being miserable, going through it living like a coward. If you want to begin to make a difference in your life, you've got to stand up for what you want that brings you a level of self-respect, self-appreciation and self-fulfillment.

Decide this day that you're going to face the things in your life that you want to change. You're more than capable of handling it. You only live one time – make it a good time!

Caption: If you want to begin to make a difference, in your life, you've got to stand up for what you want.

Success Comes In Knowing You

Do you want to become successful? What is success? What does it mean to you?

If has been said that success is getting what you want. But happiness is wanting what you get.

I know a lot of people who are in the rat race of life, every day working toward success. And I've seen them get it – that which they call success – but they found themselves miserable. Is that where you are right now?

Nancy Wilson's recording "I've Never Been to Me, " provides a reminder that many times what we're looking for is within ourselves. That which you are looking for, your living with.

Take the time to know yourself. Take personal inventory and find out today, what is it that gives your life a sense of fulfillment? Solving that mystery can truly make you happy!

Caption: ...success is getting what you want. But happiness is wanting what you get.

Cherish the People In Your Life

When was the last time you told the people in your life, people that you really value, how much you care about them, how you feel about them?

It's easy to say, "Oh they know it. I know they know it." But, when was the last time you stopped for a moment and sat them down, looked them in the eye and said, "I want you to know how much I love you, how much you mean to me." Or just wrote them a little note out of the blue, for no special occasion?

My mama used to say it's the little things in life that count. I think about that a lot. Someone I loved very much died before I had a chance to convey in words how I felt. *Surely this person knows how I felt,* kept telling myself. I've never stopped wondering whether this is entirely true.

But as I second-guessed myself about the one who passed on, I resolved to make sure those now around me know how much I appreciate them, not just for what they do, but for who they are. I don't dwell on the things that are too late to fix, but I do my best to get life's lessons and put them into action. And when it comes to my feelings, I put them into words.

Improve Yourself

James Allen's popular book, "As A Man Thinketh," pointed out that people are interested in improving their circumstances but they're unwilling to improve themselves.

As I travel around this country, speaking and putting on workshops and seminars, teaching people methods and techniques on how to develop themselves, I'm amused to see empty chairs when I look out into the audience. But if there was a concert there, you couldn't get near the place. When you talk about developing your mind, expanding your consciousness and improving yourself so that you can improve your life, you always have room. Isn't that interesting?

I'd like to share something I once heard that could help you develop your true potential: "Things are not going to get better for you until you get better. Things are not going to improve in your life, until you improve; and you are the only one who can make that happen."

Are you filling the empty spaces of opportunity in your life?

It's Not Luck

A lot of people think that when you make it in life, it's because you're lucky. I can tell you, based on my experience, that it is definitely not that kind of party.

Remember the adage: "The harder you work, the luckier you get." So if you really want to get lucky, then work hard at what you do.

It's interesting to me that most people won't do that. A lot of people are sitting around, hoping to get lucky, hoping to hit the lottery, hoping that somebody will send them some money in the mail, when everything they are wishing for only through their own efforts.

If you want things to happen in your life, then you must invest in those things. What you give is what you're going to get in return. If you don't put anything out there, don't expect anything back. But I can assure you, the better you become, the harder you work, and the more patient and relentless you are, the more rewards you will reap. Luck is nice, but work is something you can control. So get working!

Embracing Failure

Most people go through life fearing to fail. We've made failure a bad thing in our culture. In schools, we are taught that it's bad to fail.

And yet, anybody who has ever achieved anything worthwhile in life had to experience failure. You've got to make failure okay and learn from the experience.

"Don't be afraid to fail," advises H. Stanley Judd. "Don't waste energy trying to cover up failure. Learn from your failure and go on to the next challenge. It's okay to fail. If you're not failing, you're not growing."

If you want to grow and develop yourself, embrace failure. If you want to become the best at what you do, you've got to be willing to fail, again and again.

And then finally, one day, you can fail your way to greatness.

Caption: IF you want to become the best at what you do, you've got to be willing to fail, again and again.

Focus

You know why you might not be reaching your goals right now? Because you might be doing too many things. You've got too many irons in the fire.

My mama once said to me, "Son, here you are trying to do multilevel marketing, promoting concerts, photography, public relations. You're doing all these things and you also want to speak. Why don't you just pick one and do that well?" Mama was right.

Robert Collier said that you can have anything you want, if you want it bad enough. "You can be anything you want to be, have anything you desire, accomplish anything you set out to accomplish, if you will hold to that desire with singleness of purpose, "according to Collier.

Focus your energy. Find one thing and drop your buckets there. Do that one thing until it blesses you.

Complaining Doesn't Count

There are enough things wrong with the world any thinking person can find things to complain about. That takes no special genius, no great effort. There are things in our business or professional life, things in our family or home life and things in our community we could spend all day complaining about.

The problem with complaining is that some people have found a way to virtually make a living at it. They go out of their way to point out the faults others see but don't care to comment on. Or they make it a practice to offer their same complaints over and over, as though the observation is brand new and particularly insightful. They give themselves a lot of credit for doing very little.

I believe in the value of critical observations. I wouldn't be where I am, writing this book, if there hadn't been people telling me from time to time that I was off base. But complaining is something else altogether. It is as though complaining is a substitute for action. I always appreciate people who are willing to tell you what they think it wrong, but who are just as willing to tell you what they think is right, especially if they are willing to take action on the course they recommend.

If you are willing to go into action on the things you complain about, you are likely to increase your influence tenfold. Whatever facet of life you choose to complain about, be willing to back it up with action.

Some of life's greatest improvements have resulted from dissatisfaction. Be one of those who is willing to turn complaining energy into creative energy. We could all use more of that.

Caption: I always appreciate people who are willing to tell you what they think is wrong, but who are just as willing to tell you what they think is right.....

Avoiding the Shortcuts

It has been said that many of our young people become involved in selling drugs because they know they can make more doing that than they can flipping hamburgers.

If you want to make it in life – become wealthy and successful – be clear about this: There are no shortcuts! You will pay! As the Bible reminds us, "As you sow, so shall you reap." You're going to pay with your life or with time in jail, or with a life built on the shaky ground of deception.

If you want financial independence, you have to be willing to develop a skill or product or service that people want. You have to be willing to live below your means at first until you reach your goals. You have to be willing to save your money. If you want to make it today, you've got to be willing to sacrifice. You have to be willing to do what others won't do. You may have to flip a few burgers. If so, do it, and do it well.

Dig in, and expect good things, the things shortcuts won't allow you to have.

Make the Transformation

Guess who this man is. He was kidnapped as a baby. To get him back, his owners gave up a horse. Imagine that, trading a man for a horse. He went on to change the world of science.

Who was he? His name was George Washington Carver. He proved a point: that your circumstances really don't matter, that they really don't determine who you are. The only thing that matters is you.

As Elsie Robinson once said, "Things may happen around you, and things may happen to you, but the only things that really count are the things that happen in you." Regardless of your circumstances right now, I want you to know that you are bigger and better than your circumstances.

You have the power to overcome and transform your life right now.

Gaining Wisdom

Are you going through a major challenge right now? Do you find life extremely difficult today? Are you overcoming a cash-flow problem?

Remember, wisdom comes from everywhere, I am always searching for ideas that can inspire me or others to reach another level. Here's something that can perhaps impact your consciousness. You never know where it's going to come from. As country western singer Dolly Parton explains, "The way I see it, if you want the rainbow, you've got to put up with the rain."

That's powerful. James Cleveland built on that sentiment by singing, "Lord help me to hold on, 'til my change come." Who knows when my change or your change will come? We don't know. The test of faith is hanging in there where you can't see the positive outcome, only present circumstance. You have coping power you might not be aware of. I can remember situations where unpaid bills, relationship tensions, and soaring high blood pressure had me stressed and wondering if I could ever see a positive change. But getting still, looking within myself and reflecting on my faith helped me get past the challenge.

You've got to go through some difficulties. But if you hold on, you can be certain the change will come!

Caption: The test of faith is hanging in there when you can't see the positive outcome only present circumstance.

Think It

Whatever you have right now in your life is a reflection of your thoughts.

Robert Collier said that we can only have in life when we think we can have. We can only be what we think we can be. We can only do what we think we can do. We can only become what we think we can become.

Start by controlling your thoughts. We can't control the thoughts that come into our mind, but we can control what we dwell on. Start dwelling on the positive things in your life.

Judge not according to appearances. Whatever is going on in your life right now, say to yourself, *things are going to get better for me.*

Everyday and in every way, I'm getting better and better. I don't know how, but I just feel it. I just know that things are going to get better.

Thoughts have magnetic power and they will begin to attract that in your life experience.

Finding Opportunity In Crisis

A lot of people are facing some real challenges right now. Many people have been displaced from the job market, and they're wondering how to make ends meet. Some are facing challenges in their health or their home life.

Many people look at this as a crisis. Crisis in the Chinese language means danger, but it also means opportunity. It is a critical juncture, where direction and clarity are most important.

In the case of losing your job, why not view this as an opportunity the universe has given you to use your talent to do that which you love? The same is true for other situations. Bad medical news can get you on track to better health.

If you begin to think right now about how you can use your skills, your knowledge and life experiences to create some new opportunities for yourself, you'll be surprised at what comes to you.

No one can determine your destiny but you. Will it be easy? Of course not. Can you do it? Of course you can. But it requires patience and persistence. Seize this moment of crisis as your opportunity to start fresh, and live your dreams.

Making Use Of Your Talent

Now is the time for thinking. Now is the time for being creative. Now is the time to step forward and take life on. It's always the right time for these things.

There are a lot of people who have a great deal of talent that they never use.   Don't you know a lot of people who are intelligent, skillful and capable of great accomplishments, but they're holding back? Why? The first reason is fear of failure. The second reason is they don't feel they're good enough or that they're deserving.

This is the time to begin to activate the thinker in you, to begin to become the driving, active force in your life. Things have changed and you want to begin to learn how to manage change, to become the driver of change and not a victim of it. And you do that by recognizing that change is certain, even if we never quite know how or when things will change. Accept the fact that change comes and decide to take a good look for the opportunities the change will bring. Make change a tool for your success. Let it happen, and celebrate the possibilities.

Know Your Value

"You are a valuable, significant person although your circumstances may have you feeling otherwise." - JAMES W. NEWMARK

Don't define who you are and the possibilities for your life, based upon what's happening to you right now. As you begin to look at your life, ask yourself the question, *what got me here and what do I need to do to get me out of here?*

Don't begin to define your potential or the possibilities for yourself by looking at things as they are.

Follow this advice from Charles Duboise: "At any moment, we must be willing to sacrifice who we are for what we can become."

It really doesn't matter what's going on right now. The only thing that matters is what you're going to do about it. Do something powerful!

Caption: Don't define who you are and the possibilities for your life, based upon what's happening to you right now.

Giving What You've Got

If you had to determine the most important thing any of us can do right now to begin to advance our lives, I would suggest finding some way in which you could become useful in someone else's life.

Let this old saying guide you: "What you give is what you get. What you withhold from life, life withholds from you."

Many times when we spend time feeling sorry for ourselves and feeling like victims, we can turn that energy into something positive and find ways we can give something back to life.

If you cast your bread on the water – guess what – it will come back to you.

Life is challenging. Find ways in which you can begin to give more of yourself, ways in which you can begin to help others. Help somebody and help yourself because what you give is what you get.

Looking Like A Winner

If you look the part and act the part, you'll be surprised at the results you will produce. This is true with negative impressions as well as positive ones.

Are you trying to make a difference with your life? If you are, one of the things you have to do is be concerned about the energy and image you project. What you project can be either negative or positive. If you want to make a strong positive impression on someone, dress sharp, smile warmly and keep your energy level high.

We all know people who seem to want to project a negative impression. Most people don't really want to make a negative impression, they just take their image and energy so casually that they get a casual response from people. I can remember situations where I presented myself so casually that I created no real impression at all. All it took for me to change was a well placed observation from a friend who knew I had serious intentions. I later learned to match my intentions with the right suit, a nice smile, shined shoes and my best go-getter attitude.

I've heard it said that going casually through life can make you a casualty. I knew I wanted to be a winner, so I decided I would do what it takes to look like one. Don't make the mistake I made. Look and act like the winner you are.

Caption: If you want to make a strong positive impression on someone, dress sharp, smile warmly and keep your energy level high.

Gaining Control

I received a desperate call one day from a friend of mine who had been abusing herself with drugs and had spent her money to buy cocaine instead of paying her bills.

She began to cry as she told me she was on the verge of losing her home. I asked her, "Did you learn anything from this experience?" She said, "Yes." I asked her, "And what was that?" She replied, "I realize that I had given control of my life away."

How many of us have done that? Again, and again.

I asked her, "So what are you going to do now?" She replied, "I'm going to get my control back. I realize I can't do it alone. I need some help."

You are better than anything that is happening to you right now. If you're facing a challenge of drugs or alcohol or any kind of addiction, get some help. Remember that nobody can help you unless you hold on to your commitment to regain, and retain, control of your life. Like my friend, resist all temptation to backslide into the thoughts and actions that caused you to lose control in the first place.

Know that you're better than anything your facing.

Maximize Your Talent

A parent came up to me recently during one of my training sessions to tell me that her son was not doing well academically. After speaking with her, I had a chance to talk to him.

I asked him, "Why aren't you doing better in school?" And he said, "I've got a lot of other things on my mind like my music and my rap." So I explained to him that if he didn't want to end up like many celebrities and talented artists of the '50s and '60s who now have nothing to show for their accomplishments, he needed to hit the books.

If you want to make it today, talent is not enough. You must have knowledge to go along with that talent. Having knowledge helps to protect against losing any fortune you might accumulate, and education is a key to that much needed knowledge.

This is an age of awareness, an age of the mind. Those who can think or create, those who are educated or trained, those who are resourceful, those who are good business people are the ones who will determine their own destiny.

Don't allow yourself to rest on your artistic or physical skills alone. Develop and use your mind!

Positive Thinking

Psychologist William James once said that the greatest discovery of his generation was that human beings can alter their lives by altering their attitudes of mind.

There are so many people today who have defeated themselves because of their negative attitudes about themselves and about life. If you want to begin to alter your circumstances and alter your life, it's very important that you begin to change your attitude about yourself.

Begin to see the possibilities of things getting better for you. But the only way you can do that is by working to improve, to develop and to expand your consciousness. You have unlimited greatness within you. You've been endowed with greatness. It's up to you to receive it!

Caption: If you want to begin to alter your circumstances and alter your life, it's very important that you begin to change your attitude about yourself.

Create Your Circumstances

If you find yourself in the jaws of adversity, here's some good news from Benjamin Disraeli: "We're not creatures of circumstances, we are creators of circumstances."

You are made in the likeness and image of God. You've been given a power and an authority over everything on the face of this earth, including anything that you're experiencing now.

Whatever is going on, ask yourself the question, *How did I get here?* And then begin to explore, using your imagination and talking with people about solutions.

What are some of the options that you can begin to implement to get yourself out of where you are? One option is to replace worry with work. Sometimes, just digging in and working hard at one well-chosen task can make all the difference in the world. Be creative enough to redirect your energy. By going into work mode, we can focus useless energy into the useful kind. Even if the outcome of the task it not earth shaking, it puts us closer to the goal, while worry and other such mental distractions can only slow us down or stop us.

Don't waste time bathing in the negative experience. Spin your energy and focus your attention on moving on. Take the lesson from the hardship, and use it in the future. Don't just be a creature, be a creator.

Caption: Don't waste time bathing in the negative experience. Spin your energy and focus your attention on moving on.

Be Unstoppable

It amazes me every day how stoppable some people are. If you listen to the conversations of most people, you will discover the reason they don't live their dream is because they are stoppable.

Any little difficulty, any little hardship whatsoever and they're ready to immediately throw in the towel on themselves – on their dreams, on their hopes and on their aspirations.

IF you want to make something happen in life, you must be willing to stay determined, to face disappointment, to face rejection, to have people talk about you, to work against you and more. But if you want to make things happen, you've got to realize that those things don't matter at all. All that matters is you, but you can't know that if you are stoppable.

Decide that you deserve your dream enough to keep going when times get hard. Tell yourself that if it's hard, I'll do it hard. I'm unstoppable!

Get Rid of The Energy Drainers

If you want to change your destiny and the quality of your life, it's very important that you get all of the energy drainers out of your life right now.

Did you know a lot of people never realize their true potential and never reach their goals because they have not discovered the truth that some people are not good for them?

Look at the people in your life right now and write their names down. Next to their names, write down what it is that you are becoming as a result of the relationship.

Ask yourself a few crucial questions. Are you becoming a better person? Do they enhance you men tally, emotionally and spiritually? And if you find them to be a negative factor in your life, get rid of them. Get them out of your life or limit your contact immediately.

Leave energy drainers alone! Don't let them slow you down and stop your dream. Your possibilities are too important.

Be Relentless

If you've got a product or idea that you really want to be successful or if you really want to make some serious money, you've got to be relentless.

Most people don't realize that if you have something you want to do – if it's your passion, something you want to sell, some idea you want to convince someone of – you've got to talk to a lot of people before you find someone who will agree with you.

A lot of people become discouraged too soon. The name of the game is, you've got to be relentless. You've got to strike again and again and again!

Former football coaching great, the late Jake Gaither of Florida A&M University, used to say that the rattlers will strike again and again and again. And he would say that even if they were down by fifty points.

You want to reach your goal, so you've got to strike again and again and again. And I guarantee you, eventually, you will score some touchdowns of your own.

Caption: You want to reach your goal, so you've got to strike again and again and again.

It's Your Move

Where are you going? Where are you headed right now? What is the future brining you? The answer: whatever you're brining to the future!

Oliver Wendell Holmes said that the great thing in this world is not so much where we are, but where we are moving. Where are you moving right now? Is your life moving up? Or is it moving down? Whatever direction it's going, you are in control. If you want to begin to turn things around, if it's not what you want it to be, it's going to require perseverance on your part. Longfellow said that perseverance is a great element of success. If you would only knock long enough and loud enough at the gate, you are sure to wake somebody up.

If no one answered right away, just keep knocking until you wake them up. Make sure that where you are moving today is likely to get you where you want to be tomorrow. And keep moving!

Building a Case For Yourself

I was so glad to see my twin brother years ago when he returned from Iraq. I wondered if I'd ever see him again at times during the war, but it was a blessing to talk with him when he returned. And then, we had some challenges.

It's hard to reach people sometimes, especially if they are related to you. I was talking to my brother about becoming a professional speaker, like myself, and he responded by saying he couldn't do it. His response reminded me of something Robert Robottom said: "Never build a case against yourself." And that's what I told my brother Wesley. Building a case against yourself means arguing for your own demise.

So many of us do that as we go through life. Unconsciously, we start convincing ourselves why we can't do something.

I procrastinated for years because I built a strong case against myself, telling myself that I couldn't do it. If you're doing that, decide right now to change and build a case for yourself. Your greatness needs you as its strongest ally. Don't join the opposition. Be a force for your possibilities. Your greatness is at stake.

Raising Your Consciousness

Many people are talking about self-esteem, which is important as far as how people see themselves. We all need to see ourselves in a positive light. But beyond self-esteem, we need to develop a kind of consciousness that can put our self-esteem to work.

When I talk about consciousness, I'm talking about a combination of your hopes, your thoughts and your emotions, used as a force to act on what you see within yourself.

There are a lot of people who have so much talent and ability and they see themselves as being competent, but they don't have the force of a strong consciousness to activate themselves in the pursuit of their dreams.

Work every day to develop your consciousness by writing your aspirations, attending seminars, reading empowering books and articles and thinking about yourself.

As Spanish philosopher Jose Ortega y Gassett pointed out, "Our lives have at all times been before all else the consciousness of what we can do."

Make This Your Decade

Every day when you get up in the morning, you have a choice. You can get up and say, *I'm a victim and whatever happens, I can't help myself.* Or you can get up and say, *This is my decade, and mean it with every ounce of your being.*

Every day, we can either choose to be a victim or we can choose to live life victoriously. Choose ye this day, who ye will serve – your negative thoughts or you positive thoughts.

Give yourself a mental shampoo every day. When you get up in the morning, look yourself in the mirror and say, *Lord, whatever I must face today, together you and I can handle it.*

Then affirm, *this is my decade.* Then say, *I'll never, ever be broke again!* Watch how these words begin to energize you.

Caption: Every day, we can either choose to be a victim or we can choose to live life victoriously.

<u>You Deserve Only the Best</u>

Years ago, I was in Chicago riding around in a limousine with Rev. Johnnie Colemon of Christ Universal Temple, a large beautiful building that sears over 4,000 people and a ministry that has inspired people across the country. And as the limousine pulled into the driveway of the church, I asked her, "How do you account t for everything you have done?"

She replied, "Les Brown, I demand to go first-class in life." That reminded me of the poet Edwin Markham, who said, "It's a funny thing about life; if you refuse to accept anything but the best, you very often get it."

I can remember earlier in my career making my way around in a beat-up, maroon station wagon and thinking nothing about it. Third class was just fine at the time. But once I got the chance to ride in real comfort, the more I could appreciate the difference. First class is not hard to like, and I deserve it.

So many of us settle for less than what we actually deserve in life, going through life complaining, going through life talking about how bad things are, not realizing we have settled for less than we actually deserve.

Remember, you deserve the best! Go first class!

Common Ground

One of the things I like about earning my living as a public speaker is that I get to interact with all kinds of people. I have had the chance to speak with audiences across the United States and in many foreign countries, from Mexico to Switzerland and from Malaysia to Dubai. Sometimes the audiences are Americans working or traveling in foreign lands and sometimes they are locals who are facing a special challenge and sometimes they are locals who are facing a special challenge or celebrating a major accomplishment.

I love what I do because it lets me interact with a large number and wide variety of people. It also lets me know how similar people are, no matter how different their circumstances or their cultural roots. Even when I speak to non-English-speaking audiences, if the interpreter can keep up with me, I get to feel that powerful sense of oneness with the audience. And what a joy that is!

On the other hand, I've had to learn the hard way that laughter and applause come in rhythms that can throw you completely off when your punch line is delivered a few seconds later by the interpreter. What's really strange is to have an audience in which a portion speaks English and the rest of them do not. I find myself chuckling at the fact that they are two distinct patterns of laughter or applause. I try to go to my next thought and the second pattern of laughter hits. By that time,

I'm laughing along with them. That's right, laughing at the laughing. You make the adjustments to make impact.

I have concluded in my interaction with the planet that people who look for ways to embrace find ways to embrace, and people who look for dividing lines usually find solid ways to divide. No doubt, there is plenty of injustice and misunderstanding in the world, but sometimes we get to see people come together to find a common ground, and it reminds us that we are not so different.

I have the great fortune of being called upon to craft a message to help people find ways to work together. I find it happens best with good preparation, careful listening and some well-chosen words. My hope for a world of people who are standing fast and holding their ground is that more and more leaders will come to the fore with agendas that search for the common ground. I am convinced that if they look hard enough, they will figure out exactly where it is.

Caption: I have concluded in my interaction with the planet that people who look for ways to embrace find ways to embrace, and people who look for dividing lines usually find solid ways to divide.

Family Means Forgiveness

Hard times do a good job of reminding us what is important in life. Routine matters and petty issues seem to take a back seat when the going gets tough. Family and friends get to be a higher priority than they normally are. It makes you wonder: if they are so important in crunch time, how can they get so far out of focus during other times?

Families are who we are, after all. They are a looking glass, and in the best of cases, they can be a source of empowerment and support for getting the things we want out of life. Unfortunately, the family also represents a source of potential conflict. My twin brother and I competed for Mama's approval for virtually all of our lives, and it wasn't always fun and games. I know other wins who went years without speaking to each other.

They finally got together after September 11. They made contact and reconnected after years of being apart. They had turned their backs on each other over a dispute involving a man they were competing for. They had remained distant because neither would make the move to make something positive happen. They decided to make amends, because they realized in a moment of crisis that they needed each other.

They found out as I did that you have to allow the people you care most about to just be who they are.

I've done my bit of trying to fix people, and I've been on the other end. Being the fixer was okay, but being the fixee is never any fun. I suspect it works out best for all concerned when we decide to just accept each other. It's not rocket science; it's common sense. Maybe we can do a little more to make it common practice.

Caption: Families are who we are, after all. They are a looking glass, and in the best of cases, they can be a source of empowerment and support for getting the thing we want out of life.

Give Up the Baggage

The more people I talk to, the more I am convinced that the baggage we carry around from some past event represents one of the biggest challenges between us and our achievements, or our happiness. I can remember thinking about something somebody said that hurt my feelings, getting more and more bitter, long after it made any sense to be upset. I gave myself way too much pity for time.

The worst part is that it often involves something with no bad intentions; just a mindless slip, and the hate is on. I've seen people pout on and on about things that were said lightly or thoughtlessly but where clearly no disrespect was intended. Sometimes we need to just get a grip, and get over ourselves.

I've found that as I've gotten older I travel best with light baggage, so it behooves me to let the stuff from the past be in the past. I am less likely to keep score when it looks as though we all have a chance to win. So I speak up on the things that matter, and sidestep a lot of stuff that doesn't seem to have my name on it. Chicago's Rev. Johnnie Colemon says what you think about me is none of my business, and I agree. If it keeps me from being the best Les Brown, I'll just have to let it go..

If you're carrying some baggage around that won't help you get where you're trying to go, give it up. We could all be the better for it.

Be a Victor, Not a Victim

When I talk to people who are facing some special challenge, I try to get them to focus on the things that can take them where they want to go, rather than the things that are likely to keep them where they are. I found out early in life that I had to choose how to look at things. It isn't necessarily easy, but neither is life.

As an adoptee, raised by a single woman with very little education or financial means, labeled educable mentally retarded and put back from the fifth grade to the fourth, and tracked into a dead-end education, I was discovered and liberated by Leroy Washington. He was a high school drama teacher who would not let me accept the label and the stigma other had placed on me.

I hold no animosity toward my birth mother. She led me to Mamie Brown, the only mother I ever needed, and she insisted that my twin brother and I kept together. I didn't know we were poor until we weren't so poor anymore. In fact, I was too busy enjoying my childhood to notice I was missing anything. And the teacher who turned me on to myself more than made up for the one who sent me to the slow kids class.

Later, when I lost my job in broadcasting, it led me to run successfully for the state legislature, winning reelection twice. How can I let other people hand on to things, when I know the value of putting things into perspective and moving on? The fact is that I can't control what life hands me. What I can control is how I handle it.

It takes practice to be able to see things in the most useful light, but I wouldn't be Mamie Brown's son if I couldn't handle the hand I'm dealt. I don't just want to adjust, I want to rise as a victor rather than suffer as victim, and claim whatever God has in store for me. If it works for you, let it work.

Caption: …I can't control what life hands me. What I can control is how I handle it.

God's Opportunity

A lot of people go through life thinking they are going to avoid pain and struggle. Unfortunately, they will learn the hard way that there is no life without pain and struggle. The challenge is to handle pain and struggle, so you can enjoy pleasure and joy.

As you face this day, think about the words of Charles Udall, who said, "In life you will always be faces with a series of God-ordained opportunities, brilliantly disguised as problems and challenges."

If you're going through a major challenge right now, view it as a God-ordained opportunity. Know that you are more than capable of handling it. Look at it and find the blessing in it. Look at it and see how it can begin to empower you and be a catalyst in your life to take you to higher levels.

Here's wishing you Godspeed!

<u>Making Things Happen</u>

Since I've made it known that this book is actually to be put to use, this section is designed to help you put into motion that one special idea, goal or project that seems to draw you to it. The series of questions which follow will help you to map out your course for success.

What special thing would you like to achieve (obtain or complete) in the next few years, which would give you a great feeling of accomplishment?

What will it take from you to reach that point of accomplishment?

What do you believe has kept you from achieving your goal so far? (Why haven't you achieved it already?)

What strengths will you be able to call upon to take you to your goal?

What weaknesses will you need to overcome or minimize, so that they won't hold you back?

What strategy will you use, or what will you tell yourself, when you have a setback or disappointment?

Who can you call upon now to support you in your efforts?

How will you attract additional support, if needed, to get to your goal?

Which of the "Up Thoughts" will you see to get over some of the rough spots you will undoubtedly face in pursuing your goal?

What are some of the other sources you will use when you are facing a low point or an uphill challenge? (Include religious texts, poems, photos, quotes, music, etc.)

<u>Other Products</u>

Get more from Les Brown, the motivator. Order his books and audio-visual tools today by visiting his online store at www.lesbrown.com or by calling 1-800-733-4226.

Audio Collections

Choosing Your Future (with or without workbook)

Speaking Your Way to Unlimited Wealth Vols: 1 & 2 (with or without the workbook)

It's Not Over Until I Win

Create Your Greatest Life

Leadership

Books

It's Not Over Until You Win!

Live Your Dreams

Video Collection

It's In Your Hands!

You Deserve!

It's Possible!

The Power To Change

Live Your Dreams...Get Past Your Fears!

Take Charge of Your Life!

Live Full, Die Empty

How To Tell Your Story